THE
DEAN WITTER
GUIDE TO
PERSONAL
INVESTING

BY
ROBERT M. GARDINER

A SIGNET BOOK

SIGNET
Published by the Penguin Group
Penguin Books USA Inc., 375 Hudson Street,
New York, New York 10014, U.S.A.
Penguin Books Ltd, 27 Wrights Lane,
London W8 5TZ, England
Penguin Books Australia Ltd, Ringwood,
Victoria, Australia
Penguin Books Canada Ltd, 10 Alcorn Avenue,
Toronto, Ontario, Canada M4V 3B2
Penguin Books (N.Z.) Ltd, 182–190 Wairau Road,
Auckland 10, New Zealand

Penguin Books Ltd, Registered Offices:
Harmondsworth, Middlesex, England

Published by Signet, an imprint of Dutton Signet,
a division of Penguin Books USA Inc.

The Dean Witter Guide to Personal Investing previously appeared in an NAL
Books edition published by New American Library. The hardcover edition was
published simultaneously in Canada by The New American Library of Canada
Limited.

First Signet Printing, February, 1989
11   10

 REGISTERED TRADEMARK—MARCA REGISTRADA

Printed in the United States of America

PUBLISHER'S NOTE

This publication is designed to provide accurate and authoritative information in
regard to the subject matter covered. It is sold with the understanding that the
publisher is not engaged in rendering legal, accounting, or other professional
service. If legal advice or other expert assistance is required, the service of a
competent professional person should be sought.

CONTENTS

v

Preface to the Signet Edition

As I traveled around the country following the initial publication of this book, I found a lot of people with bad cases of the shakes. The stock market collapse of October 1987 had shocked them. They were reluctant to invest their money in stocks, and they were worried about the future of the American economy. Was inflation coming back? Was a recession inevitable? Was the market going to crash again? Many individual investors were so distressed by these questions that they had taken their money and put it back "under the mattress." That is, they had put it in secure but low-yielding places like savings accounts and certificates of deposit. They were nervous, so they were playing it safe.

And they were costing themselves a lot of money.

Now, everybody *should* keep a nest egg in some sort of readily accessible and secure investment, but there is no need to shortchange oneself in doing so. At the same time that many cautious investors were putting their money into savings accounts paying just over 5 percent interest, some mutual funds holding nothing but iron-clad government bonds were paying almost twice that rate.

Investors with more tolerance for risk could have found excellent values in the stock market. IBM, for example, reached a high of 175 during 1987, then fell to 102. At 175, it was certainly overpriced. But at 102 it was just as certainly underpriced. In a prime example of stock market irrationality, people who had thronged to but the stock at 170 wouldn't touch it at 110—yet nothing about the company had changed except the price. As I write, IBM stands at 125, and I'm willing to bet that its long-term trend will be an upward one.

Over the long term, the trend of American stock—and the American economy—has *always* been an upward one. As we enter the 1990s, I have yet to encounter any good reason to believe that trend will change.

This is not to say that everything will be great everywhere. We seem to have entered a curious type of economic cycle in which the economy does not rise or fall as a whole but rises or falls in spots. In recent years, we have seen most of the country boom while Texas fell into recession. The stocks of service companies soared while those of "smokestack" industries were dead as smelts.

The one great truth of all cycles is that they go round. What has been down will come up; what has been up will falter. Texas real estate will not be in the pits forever. Our smokestack industries are already showing strong signs of revitalization.

Overall, the American economy will continue to grow. It may increase 4 percent a year, or maybe only 2 percent, but wealth will continue to be created in this contry, and the publicly owned corporations that create that wealth will be rewarded with increased sales and profits. Shareowners of those companies will be rewarded in turn with increased dividends and higher share prices.

At least, that will be the *long-term* trend. I have seen that trend persist during my forty years in the stock market, and I expect ot see it continue. Of course, the market will go up and the market will go down. It always does. I even expect that we may see some dramatic drops in the market (although mechanisms are now in place to make the next drop less drastic than the last). But, as we move through the 1990s, I expect each successive high to be higher than its predecessor, and each low to be a little less low.

During the lows, as always, investors will become demoralized, and there will consequently be great bargains to be had by the stouthearted. One of the most dismaying things I have seen in recent months is the flight from the stock market by individual investors. When nobody wants to buy stocks is precisely the time to be buying, not fleeing.

A lot of publicity about computerized "program trading" and the like has contributed to scaring small investors out of the stock market. They feel that mighty institutions dominate the game and that the little guy can't get a fair break. But the institutions, in many cases, have feet of clay. The managers of pension funds and other vast pools of capital are often graded, from quarter to quarter, on their short-term performance and may be fired if they fall behind. This has made some of them so obsessed with the short-term perormance of their investments that they buy and sell in complicated, choreographed routines, prompted by technical factors like disparities in price between shares of stock and stock futures that have nothing to do with the *underlying value* of the securities they are trading. Individuals who are investing in sound stocks for the long term, with no self-imposed pressure for short-term gains, can take advantage of the institutions' irrationality. By buying stocks when the institutions are dumping them, the individual can come out ahead.

As for the great bogey of the early 1980s—inflation—I think we are safe from it. The cost of living will certainly fluctuate, but if it starts to go too high, it will be stomped back down. Our political leaders have learned how to control inflation. It is a painful cure, but the American public will accept it, or even demand it, in preference to the alternative.

If I sound like an optimist, so be it. I have been bullish all my life—through recessions, depression, wars, and scandals—and it has worked for me. I see nothing worse on the horizon than I have already seen. I see nothing to change my mind now.

ACKNOWLEDGMENTS

Writing this book was a collaborative process involving many people both within and without the Sears Financial Network. But it began within, at Dean Witter, with my colleague Donna Peterman, who conceived this project and shepherded it through many difficulties. Without Donna, there would have been no book.

For generously contributing their insights on investing, I am deeply indebted to Carl Hulick and William Hurt. Others whose expertise is reflected here include Ned Oelsner, Grant Somerville, and Terry Fuller of Dean Witter; Joe Hanauer and Ted Patrick of Coldwell Banker; Fred Hansen of Allstate; and my former colleague Robert Stovall. Brian Fallon provided valuable research assistance. Catherine Simmons-Gill, Jim Howard, and Louise Otten furnished legal and administrative support.

In the publishing world, a different kind of market than the one I am used to, our agent, Amanda Urban, guided this book to the best bidder. LuAnn Walther, our editor at New American Library, had the wit to acquire the manuscript at a propitious moment and has been encouraging throughout.

Finally, I want to acknowledge the contribution of Ed Zuckerman, an experienced journalist who converted the ideas of my colleagues and myself into lively prose. The best advice in the world is useless if it's too boring to read. Ed made sure that wasn't the case here.

PREFACE

On April 1, 1946, I began my career in the securities business. The stock market, at the time, was in the midst of a post-World War II rally. The Dow Jones Industrial Average hit the then-dizzying peak of 212.50. All was wine and roses.

And then the market collapsed. Before the year was over, the Dow Jones fell to 163. Wall Street was overtaken by gloom.

The gloom lasted for a long time. The market did not reach its 1946 peak again until 1950. But during those down years, as young and green as I was, I knew one thing: there were bargains to be had. In fact, you could have picked them with your eyes closed. All you had to do was select from a list of quality companies—and wait. They would go up again.

And they did. The market boomed through most of the 1950s—as it has boomed following every slump in history (and slumped following every boom). This is what some people forgot following the market "meltdown" of October 1987: the market goes up and the market goes down, but—in the long run—it goes up.

Back in 1946, not too many Americans were worried about the stock market, because only a handful of people owned shares of stock.

Brokerage houses were not oriented toward, nor interested in, the small investor. Stock exchange rules required brokers with ground-floor offices to paint their windows black. They needed special permission to put up displays. Drop-in customers were clearly not expected—or invited.

As recently as a decade or so ago, the stock market was dominated by wealthy individuals and large institutions. Individuals who were less than rich were shut out as well from other types of investment opportunities that were available to their millionaire cousins. There were no money market funds, no central asset accounts, no Individual Retirement Accounts. When it came to life insurance, consumers had their choice of whole life or term, take it or leave it. Mutual funds were available with only a limited variety of investments and investment objectives.

In the mid-1970s, you were either rich, or you kept your money in a low-interest savings account and a no-interest checking account. There wasn't much else you could do with it.

Then came the high-inflation years of the late 1970s. People learned very quickly that keeping their money in fixed-interest savings accounts was a sure way to lose ground. Their savings grew so slowly that they were actually *losing* money even while they saved. So they began to look for ways to make their money work harder.

Their search coincided with a wave of deregulation in the financial services industry. Gaps were broken in the artificial barriers separating banks, securities brokers, and insurance companies. The more aggressive of those institutions took advantage of the opportunity to compete for investors' dollars by offering new, higher-yielding investment vehicles, both within and without their former areas of specialization. Within a few years, the landscape of American investments changed forever. There are now dozens of ways—and places—for individuals and families to put their money to work at attractive rates of return.

Among those coming face to face with this profusion of choices are millions of new investors who have only recently entered the financial markets. They are members of the baby-boom generation, now entering their peak earning years. They are recent retirees, now taking personal control of pension dollars previously managed by pension funds. They are individuals from all age groups who have built up nest eggs in their Individual Retirement Accounts and are now ready to place that money in higher-yielding investments than the money market funds and certificates of deposit they began with.

These new investors are more sophisticated than the new investors of years past. They learned a lesson from the high-inflation era of the late 1970s. They have gained some experience in the financial world from their IRAs. They are committed to self-reliance; they don't want to be dependent on Social Security in their retirement years. They are prepared to compare alternative investment vehicles and to choose among them intelligently.

Many have chosen the stock market. In the last decade, the number of shareholders in American corporations has nearly doubled, from 25 million to 47 million. Others have chosen some of the new investment vehicles that did not even exist a decade ago. Still others are still trying to decide among the bewildering array of choices available to them.

Here at Dean Witter, I believe we have done more than any other brokerage firm in America to help these new investors make their choices. As I look around at all the financial service companies that target the affluent few, I am reminded of the modern Indian guru who said, "So many religions look after the poor. Leave the rich to me." Dean Witter has always followed a different path. Ever since its founding in 1924, the firm has been dedicated to individual customer service. This was a guiding principle of Mr. Dean Witter himself, who once declared, "In the long run those firms which survive and prosper are those who maintain conservative policies and put their customers' interests first." In 1981, when Dean Witter became part of Sears, Roebuck and Co., it took a big step forward in providing its services to the new investors who needed them. It brought the securities business to the general public, which is where I for one believe it belongs.

There were, of course, jokesters who derided the idea that Sears customers would "buy their stocks where they buy their socks," but the Sears Financial Network centers in Sears stores have been a resounding success. They have brought new business to Dean Witter while they have brought a complete range of investment opportunities to millions of consumers who might not otherwise have had them. (And a note to the Wall Street skeptics who looked down their noses at the Sears customer: The average income of clients opening brokerage accounts at Sears Financial Network centers has been equal to that of all stockholders nationwide.)

One thing the doubters overlooked was Sears' long experience in the financial marketplace. Sears began making consumer loans to its customers in 1911. The banks of the time wouldn't do it, so Sears stepped into the breach with unsecured loans to enable families to buy big-ticket items.

That lending evolved into the Sears credit card, which made Sears the largest retail lender in the United States. In 1931, Sears created Allstate Insurance, now the second-largest property and casualty company in the nation and a leader in life insurance as well. In 1981, Sears acquired Coldwell Banker, the nation's biggest full-service real estate firm. In 1986, it launched the Discover bank credit card.

Dean Witter has, historically, been a conservative firm. (During the Great Depression, when other firms struggled and died, Dean Witter made a profit every year, because it had refrained from imprudent speculation during the feverish boom that preceded the great crash.) Today, we offer investments that are secure enough even for our most cautious clients yet pay competitive interest rates. Clients with a higher tolerance for risk—and *only* those clients—have their choice of investments offering higher rates of return. In all cases, it is in the interests of the Dean Witter broker to conserve his or her client's capital. Our brokers do not earn commissions only by buying and selling securities. They are also rewarded for growth in their clients' money fund and mutual fund balances and other steady accumulations of wealth.

My own background is in the securities business. I began as a lowly research analyst with A. M. Kidder & Company and had worked my way up to become chairman of Reynolds Securities by 1978, when Reynolds merged with Dean Witter (three years before Dean Witter Reynolds merged with Sears). My years in the brokerage business have given me a good feeling about stocks, despite the ups and downs of the market. (I explain why in Chapter 6.) I believe that investors of even modest means can do well for themselves with stocks. I have seen many do so.

But there is a whole world of other investments out there, many with their own distinct advantages. I have drawn on the knowledge and experience of colleagues throughout Dean Witter and the Sears Financial Network to include them in this book.

We have no ax to grind. Collectively, the members of the Sears Financial Network offer almost every type of investment available anywhere, from money market funds to oil-and-gas limited partnerships, from municipal bonds to gold coins. All we insist upon is that all our clients—and potential clients—are better off with *some type* of investment or savings program.

This book is offered to guide you toward the one that is best for you.

CHAPTER 1

THE SLOW ROAD
TO RICHES

DRIFTING ALONG

People drift along. From paycheck to paycheck, they take care of their bills and put gas in the car. When they have a few extra dollars, they go out to dinner and catch a show.

Most everybody has a savings account—and outstanding credit card bills to offset it. Everybody knows they're covered by Social Security (although they may have doubts as to whether the Social Security system will be ready for them when they're ready for it). Most employees are covered by some kind of pension or profit-sharing plan, but they haven't thought too much about it. They earn their money, and they spend it to live, and life goes on.

Still, in the backs of their minds, they know they should be devoting some serious thought to their financial affairs. How will they send the kids to college? What will they live on in their old age? How can they take the best advantage of money market funds, Independent Retirement Accounts, and the whole gamut of new financial arrangements that has been created in the last decade or so? (Not to mention tax-free municipal bonds, zero-coupon bonds, mutual funds, real estate investments, stocks, annuities, new forms of life insurance . . . the list goes on.) It takes time to learn about these things, and most people don't have much extra time. So the weeks go by, and then the years, and people live their lives with a vague but constant worry that, someday, they're not going to have enough money.

It doesn't have to be this way. Anyone who can earn a decent living and knows how to add, multiply, and divide (or, failing that, how to work a calculator) can do a whole lot better than just get by. People with unexceptional incomes can, without great hardship, make arrangements to guarantee their future financial security. They can, in fact, accumulate small fortunes. (That is, if you consider several hundred thousand dollars to be a small fortune. I do.) There is nothing magical about the process, and it does not require great luck or great skill. It does, however, require planning and discipline. And it requires that you give up any idea you might have that you can get rich quick. You can't. But you *can*, if you want to, get rich slowly. Wouldn't you be foolish not to try?

SANTA CLAUS IS DEAD

A stockbroker I know, when he was just starting out, kept a neat little notebook full of information about his clients and prospects, just as beginning stockbrokers are supposed to. Whenever he met with a new client, he would take out his notebook and dutifully ask, "Why do you want to invest?"

"To make money," the client would reply, and he would look at the broker doubtfully. Why on earth did this joker *think* he wanted to invest? To while away the lazy afternoons?

"That's fine," said the broker, and he would write "to make money" on the appropriate line in his notebook. (Pretty soon he had an entire notebook filled with clients whose investment goals were "to make money.")

The broker's next question was, "How much money do you want to make?"

The clients' answers varied, but they rarely put any limit on how much they wanted to make. What their answers boiled down to was, "All the money in the world."

"Well," the broker would say, "I'm afraid one of us is going to be disappointed then. Because that's my goal too, and we can't both make it. Would you perhaps settle for $100 million?"

The broker finally realized, however, that his clients didn't really want all the money in the world, and they didn't even really want $100 million. What they wanted, in fact, was no specific amount of money at all. What they wanted was a *feeling*.

I call that feeling "financial serenity."

Financial serenity is a state of mind. It comes over people when they have achieved a standard of living with which they are comfortable, and when they have enough net worth to maintain that standard of living for the rest of their lives. Things might get even better, but that's not the most important point. The most important point is that things are never going to get worse.

Financial serenity is really another way of describing financial independence. It means that a person has enough money set aside, has enough money working for her (or him), that she doesn't have to count on anything beyond her control. She doesn't have to fear a recession or a business downturn. She doesn't have to pray that little Jerome, who never was too good at English, will win a college scholarship. She doesn't have to work after retirement if she doesn't want to. She doesn't have to rely on Social Security or any other government or personal assistance to provide her with a respectable living in her old age.

You can achieve financial independence if you want to. You can enjoy the cozy feeling of financial serenity, with nagging little doubts about the future forever banished. If you don't achieve financial serenity, it will be for a very simple reason: You didn't try. You won't be alone in that. Few people try. Instead, they develop elaborate rationalizations for why they aren't trying. They blame their parents, who failed to leave them an inheritance. They talk about how the little guy doesn't have a chance in the financial markets, so why bother. Or they procrastinate, promising that next week, next year, after the next raise, they will begin to put a little something away.

Or, sometimes, they try one thing. They buy a stock they hear about from Uncle Fred, or they take a flyer in the commodities market. And the stock goes down ("You didn't actually *buy* that stock, did you?" says Uncle Fred), or it's a bad year for pork bellies, and they give up in disgust. But that isn't really trying. That's gambling. That's looking for lightning to strike. That's following a rainbow.

I have some very sad news for these people, and it may be sad news for you too. I know many very intelligent people who have a hard time accepting it. Or they say they accept it, but they still handle their finances as if they'd never heard it.

This is the bad news:

There is no Santa Claus.

This is a sad fact that most people learned with shock and sorrow when they were five years old. Yet it never ceases to amaze me how many intelligent, tough-minded, successful people keep trying to revive Santa Claus in their approach to investing.

Well, forget it. Santa Claus really is dead. Write that down and stick it on your refrigerator door. If a deal looks too good to be true, it is. If someone tells you you can make a thousand dollars a week stuffing envelopes at home or stockpiling selenium in your basement, he's exaggerating. If Uncle Fred gives you some hot news about a stock that's sure to go up, ask yourself: Why am I one of the few people in America privileged to hear this news? Why do I know something that many brilliant people who spend their entire lives studying the investment scene do not know? The answer is, you don't. By the time you hear any hot news, it is cold, and it is already reflected in the price of the stock. (If you actually did have access to wonderful—and legal—information, you would already be rich and you wouldn't be reading this book. If you're reading this book anyway, give me a call. Let's have lunch.)

THE IMPOSSIBLE QUEST

Even without the dubious advantage of allegedly hot news, many people go into the investment arena looking for $10 investments that will go to $15 in six months. They may never actually define their goal to themselves that way, but that is what it amounts to. They assume they are being quite reasonable and undemanding to set as a standard finding a $10 stock, say, that will go to $15 in six months. After all, that calls for upward movement of less than one point a month. Shouldn't a reasonably astute selection be able to provide this?

No.

What such people are seeking, defined another way, is a 50 percent return on their investment every six months. If you found such a stock (at $10 a share) and put $10,000 into it, you would be able to sell it six months later (at $15 a share) for $15,000. If you promptly reinvested that in another $10 stock that went to $15 in six months, you could sell that out for $22,500. A very nice profit for a year's work.

Reinvest that in another $10 stock that goes to $15, and then do it again, and at the end of the second year you would have $50,625. At the end of the third year you would have $113,906. After six years you would be a millionaire. After fifteen years you would be a billionaire. After twenty-two years you would be able to pay off a typical annual deficit of the United States government, if you were feeling generous. Just three years after that (if you decided not to pay off the deficit after all) your wealth would exceed the total value of all the stocks listed on the New York Stock Exchange.

By this time, you would be a trillionaire. In another three or four years, you would own all the wealth on earth. Congratulations.

Do you still think it is reasonable to look for $10 stocks that will go to $15 in six months? You might find one once in a while, of course. But you can't find them all the time, and you can't find one any single time for certain. If you could consistently spot $10 stocks that went to $15—not in six months but in a year, or even two—then IBM would be very happy to sell off its computer business and give you its money to invest on its behalf.

THE POWER OF COMPOUND INTEREST

You may have noticed something interesting about the growth of that $10,000 stake to a sum greater than the wealth of the world. In the first few years, the amount of money involved grew at a substantial but not unimaginable rate. Then it soared. This is an example of compound interest in action. That $10,000 was growing at an annual rate of 100 percent, compounded twice a year. That is, interest was paid on the original principal (the $10,000), and thereafter interest was paid on the principal and the accumulated interest as well. The same thing happens in your savings account, although not quite so dramatically. If you have $100 in a bank that pays 5 percent interest, and that interest is compounded once a year, at the end of one year you will have $105 (your original $100 plus $5 interest). At the end of the second year, you will have not just $110 ($105 plus another $5 interest); you will have $110.25. You will have received interest on your original $100 and also on the interest you accumulated during the first year.

After three years your $100 will grow to $116 (rounding off to the nearest dollar). After five years you will have $128. After ten years, $163. Twenty years, $265. Thirty years, $432.

Not bad, but what if you could earn 10 percent on your money? After one year you would have $110 instead of $105. Not much difference. After twenty years, however, instead of $265 you would have $673. After thirty years, instead of $432 you would have $1,745. All from an initial investment of $100. A few percentage points up or down in the interest rate, over time, makes all the difference in the world.

There is no way you are going to earn a steady 100 percent on any investment (by finding $10 stocks that go to $15 in six months), but there is no reason to settle for 5 percent either. Somewhere between the interest rate your bank will pay you and the interest rate Santa Claus would pay you (if he existed, which he doesn't) there is a very nice rate of return that you can reasonably expect to earn in a well-conceived investment program. It is not at all farfetched, for example, to look for—and find—$20 stocks that go to $21 in a year and pay a $1 dividend, or an equivalent investment in bonds or real estate.

That's a 10 percent return, and 10 percent can do nice things for you. If, starting at the age of thirty, you put $150 a month into an investment program that earns a steady 10 percent, at age sixty-five you will have $574,242.[1] No tricks. No mirrors. You set aside some money. It grows. And then the growth grows. In 1748, Benjamin Franklin, who was a big fan of compound interest, described it like this: "Money is of a prolific, generating nature. Money can beget money, and its offspring can beget more." You're not going to argue with Benjamin Franklin, are you?[2]

---

[1] What about taxes, you say. Won't the compounding be reduced because part of each year's interest is taken by the taxman? Not necessarily. There are several entirely legal and increasingly popular ways to defer all taxes on such capital growth until retirement, even under the new tax law.

[2] Upon his death in 1790, Franklin put his money where his mouth was. He bequeathed $4,600 apiece to the cities of Boston and Philadelphia for charitable purposes, with the instruction that they were to lend out the money at interest for one hundred years before they gave any of it away. Boston's inheritance grew to $332,000 by 1890. The city built a school with part of the money and put the rest of it back to work.

INVESTING VS.
PLAYING THE LOTTERY

In the last few years, state lotteries have become popular in the United States. The big prize is often announced as $1 million. At candy stores and newsstands across the nation, millions of Americans plunk down a dollar or two every week, week after week, dreaming of winning that million-dollar prize.

The million-dollar prize, however, really doesn't amount to $1 million. Lottery officials do not hand the winner $1 million checks. They hand them checks for $50,000 and promise to hand them another $50,000 every year for twenty years. Twenty times $50,000 does equal $1 million, but getting $50,000 each year for twenty years is a far different thing, and worth far less, than getting $1 million dollars in a lump sum.

If lottery officials were to invest $500,000 at 10 percent interest, they would have $50,000 every year to give to a million-dollar winner, and at the end of twenty years they could have their $500,000 back. If they didn't care about getting their money back at the end, they could give away part of the principal every year along with the interest, working things out so that on the day the last check was due, there remained exactly $50,000 in the investment fund. To set up such a fund at 10 percent interest would cost $425,700. That, not $1 million, is what it costs a state lottery to give away a "million-dollar" prize.

If you had $425,700, you could set up your own fund and give yourself a check for $50,000 a year for twenty years. And, as I showed above, you *can* have $425,700 if you want to. Putting aside $150 a month from ages thirty to sixty-five at 10 percent interest will produce a fund of $574,242, which would put you in a *better* position than somebody who won a million-dollar lottery. You can have $425,700, the exact equivalent of winning a million-dollar lottery, if you set aside $111 a month. You probably have $111.

By the way, if you were to put just $2 a week into an investment program instead of using it to buy lottery tickets, at age sixty-five you would have $33,349. You could then start drawing out $64 a week for the rest of your life without ever touching the principal. This isn't quite a million dollars, but you don't have to have six Ping-Pong balls with your numbers on them come up to get it. And there doesn't have to be a Santa Claus to give it to you. Just a human being (you) taking sensible steps on the road to financial serenity.

CHAPTER 2

GETTING STARTED

YOUR CURRENT INVESTMENT PROGRAM

Okay, you say, the idea of starting an investment program sounds just fine. But at the moment I'm a little strapped for cash. Or, I've got too much going on right now to take the time to figure out exactly what to do. Or, I'm not sure I'm ready to start an investment program quite yet. So, for a while anyway, I'm not going to do a thing.

That's where you're wrong. You're already doing something. Doing nothing is doing something. Doing nothing means you've decided that the way you're handling your money right now is the way you will continue to handle your money.

And you are handling money, probably quite a bit. If you're earning just $25,000 a year, and expect to earn that much or its equivalent for the rest of your working life,

17

your lifetime income will be more than $1 million. A million dollars will pass through your hands, and you're going to have to manage it somehow. You're *already* managing it. In fact, you already have an investment program. You may not call it that, but it's there. Part of your income is going to Social Security. You may have a company pension plan, or a payroll savings plan. You're paying an insurance premium. You're making mortgage payments. You have some money in the bank. This is an investment program. It's probably not the one you would choose if you sat down and looked at all the alternatives, but you *have* chosen it, by default.

Every day that you do nothing to rearrange your finances, you are saying implicitly, "There is nothing I can do to improve my financial position." This is almost certainly not true. You might, for example, have a substantial sum in a savings account paying 5¼ percent interest, or even in a checking account paying no interest at all. You have it there because it's convenient and safe, and you can get to it to cover both regular expenses and possible emergencies. But, as we saw during the high-inflation era of the late 1970s, money in bank accounts can actually dwindle away. A dollar in a 5 percent savings account during a period of 10 percent inflation is worth only 95 cents at the end of a year. A dollar in a no-interest checking account (or in a coffee can under the bed) is worth even less.

Everybody should have *some* money in liquid assets (that is, assets that are readily available for spending), but there are safe, convenient money market accounts—many of which you can write checks on—that pay higher interest rates than savings accounts. You can have your money in stocks or a mutual fund, and keep up with inflation or more, and still be able to sell out quickly (or borrow with your securities as collateral) if you ever need cash for an emergency. It is incredible to me, therefore, that Americans still keep $376 billion in low-interest savings accounts. Holding more than you need for day-to-day expenses in a savings or checking account is simply throwing money away, often in exchange for no extra safety or convenience.

Many people have accumulated cash values in life insurance policies. The insurance companies are paying them negligible interest on that money. They can often borrow it back from the insurance companies at relatively low rates and reinvest it elsewhere for a riskless profit. Yet they don't do it, because they haven't had a chance (they say) to start an investment program yet.

Other people invested in stocks at some time in the past and then put them aside for long-term growth or continuing income. But things change. Stocks that looked good ten years ago may be only mediocre investments today. Other stocks may have stronger growth possibilities, or might by paying higher dividends. I recall looking at portfolios a couple of years ago and seeing a lot of oil company stocks. It was great to own oil stocks in the mid- to late 1970s, when there was rapid inflation and the value of the companies' oil reserves was appreciating to keep up with it. But, by the early 1980s, inflation had slowed down. The price of oil was dropping. Some oil stocks were still good investments, but, when I saw an individual with a whole slew of them, I knew I was looking at an out-of-date portfolio. (A couple of years later, by the way, when oil prices bottomed out, the price of oil stocks had dropped to the point where they were once again a very good buy.)

Investment inventories have to be managed the way a wine lover manages her cellar or an orchard owner his trees. Drink the mature bottles before they turn; prune the branches. You have got to examine your holdings on a regular basis and ask, "If I had the current market value of these investments in cash, would I buy the same investments back?" Sometimes the answer to that question is yes, but often it is no. If it's no, then you should act. If you wouldn't buy those investments back if you had their value in cash, then you shouldn't have them at all. (It's just a matter of a phone call to a broker to turn those investments into cash.) It doesn't matter what you paid for your holdings in the first place, either. If you bought a stock at $10 and it dropped to $5, you might be waiting for it to go back up. But why *should* it go back up? In reality, there is no reason in the world why it is any more likely to go from $5 to $10 than any other $5 stock. Your stock doesn't "remember" that it used to be at $10. There is no physical force drawing it back up to $10 because it once occupied that lofty position. At $5 a share, it might be a good investment and worth holding, or it might not. But making that decision should have nothing to do with what it used to sell for.

YOUR CURRENT ASSETS (HIDDEN AND OTHERWISE)

Before you can go anywhere at all, you have to know where you are and where you want to go. This sounds as if it should be too elementary to mention, but many people flounder in wrong directions because, financially speaking, they never stopped to figure out which way is up.

What is your starting position? What is your net worth? That is, how much more do you own than you owe? Odds are, it's greater than you think.

When it comes to totalling up your assets, listing items

like stocks and bonds and bank accounts is obvious. But what about your house? Many people tend to value a house at the amount of money they've put into it, or the amount they have so far paid off on their mortgage. The actual value of your house, however, is what you can *sell* it for, not what you paid for it. Its market value, minus the amount you owe on it, is your house's contribution to your net worth.

Other assets that are sometimes overlooked are those held in payroll savings plans, the cash value of life insurance policies, security deposits on rented property, and vested interests in pension plans. (The latter are especially valuable assets, because they shelter current contributions from taxes and grow tax-free until retirement.)

Looking toward retirement, there is also the value of your expected Social Security benefits. There has been a lot of loose talk lately about the unsoundness of the Social Security system. It is indeed a fact that the money you pay into Social Security today is not set aside to pay you benefits when you retire. Instead, it is paid right out to today's retirees. But there is no reason to think that this sort of system will not continue indefinitely. In all civilized societies, some wealth is transferred from working people to those who are too old or otherwise unable to work. The system here may be adjusted and modified, but it is not very likely that American society ten, twenty, or thirty years from now will simply tell its elder members to go starve to death. (All questions of decency aside, the political power of older voters also lends security to Social Security.) One can rely on some sort of government pension as long as the United States manages to stay a step or two above cannibalism, and that pension can be the equivalent of a substantial asset. At today's rates, a typical retiree might collect $600 a month. This is the exact equivalent of owning $90,000 worth of 8 percent government bonds.

A surprisingly large number of people can also expect to benefit someday from the natural transfer of assets that takes place as families age and elders pass away. Those who can anticipate receiving inheritances may protest that they don't want to count on that kind of thing, that they hope their parents and grandparents live a hundred years, enjoying the use of their own money all the while and leaving just enough behind to cover cabfare to the funeral home. But people tend not to play things that close. It is not at all uncommon today for average income-earners of the older generation to own fully-paid-up homes and some life insurance. With even modest accumulations of savings, this often amounts to a substantial estate. A person who stands to benefit from such an estate is in a different asset position than someone who does not.

Similarly, parents of successful children have a reserve asset that may be drawn upon in hard times. In most societies of the past, children were looked upon exactly this way, as resources to provide security for one's old age. This is one reason why, even today, it is so difficult to convince poor peasants in overcrowded countries to have fewer children. (Poverty and the fear of old-age destitution thus cause overpopulation, which in turn helps cause poverty.) In America, the parents of successful children may protest that they never would take anything from their sons and daughters. Yet often those children say there is nothing that would give them more pleasure than helping their parents. Clearly, an elderly person with such children is in a better asset position than one with no children. Parents of unsuccessful children, on the other hand, may have a continuing need to share their own assets with their children.

Other hidden assets include some items that look at first glance like expenses. Education, for one, may cost tens of thousands of dollars, but that is not an expense; it is an investment. Having an education is like owning a business; your increased skills and employability are going to make you money. Similarly, spending money to raise and educate your children is an investment in human capital that may someday be valuable to you. Money spent on improving a home or buying a vacation house is not an expense but an investment in real estate (and an excellent hedge against inflation).

Even if you don't own a house and have not been to college and have neither well-off parents nor children, you still have yourself. You have a brain. You have intelligence. You have the ability to earn a living. Over your lifetime you will almost certainly earn more than $1 million. *You* are an asset.

Finally, you have an additional advantage because you had the good fortune to be born in, or the gumption to move to, a country where it is possible to accumulate wealth. In the United States, and much of the rest of the Western world, we take for granted certain prerequisites for economic success that are in short supply elsewhere. The essential stability of our government and economy give enduring value to the paper assets that are central to any investment program. In much of the world, people keep their savings in the form of gold or jewelry. They never know when their governments will fall, or their economies will collapse, or industries might be nationalized. There might be limits on their freedom to invest their money as they like or to move it from market to market. These people do what they can to protect what they have, but gold bars hidden in a chimney are not earning any interest. That kind of wealth does not grow.

In stable Western societies, it is not foolhardy to trade one's wealth for a piece of paper, such as a bond or stock certificate or savings passbook. One can have confidence that next year, and the year after that, those pieces of paper will still have value. This is the often unappreciated first prerequisite for any investment program.

Our society also provides us with a highly developed infrastructure of roads, energy distribution systems, communications, and other essential support services for business and industry. If an entrepreneur has an idea for a new product, he can open a shop and start to produce it. He doesn't have to begin by digging a well and buying a generator. Nor does he have to teach newly hired employees how to count, or even how to program a computer. Our educational system turns out millions of qualified people each year in all fields. Human capital is available for any new enterprise.

Making money in the United States is also simplified by the fact that all around you people are making money. The American economy creates wealth at a huge and exponentially expanding rate. Even during the recession years of the early 1980s, the American economy was growing at an annual rate of 1.3 percent. This means that $20 billion of new wealth was created (equal to the Gross National Product of Peru), even in a bad year.[1] In 1986 (a so-so year), the American economy grew at a real annual rate of 2.5 percent. America produced $90 billion more in goods and services than it had the year before. This wealth was apportioned among American citizens (and foreign invest-

----

[1]These figures are averages for 1980–83. During the heart of the recession (1980 and 1982), the real Gross National Product (adjusted for inflation) actually declined. Such declines have been unusual in American history.

ors) who contributed to or invested in the wealth-creation process.

Steady growth over the decades has made Americans, even those with modest incomes, wealthy in historical and international terms. Poor people from Latin America, Asia, and elsewhere risk death to sneak into the United States, where any job will make them "rich" compared to those they left behind. Americans of moderate means today enjoy luxuries that were beyond the reach of John D. Rockefeller, Sr. As rich as he was, Rockefeller could not travel from New York to Los Angeles in a few hours, in a vehicle that was cooled on an uncomfortably hot day, all the while dining on out-of-season tropical fruit and listening to the New York Philharmonic Orchestra play whatever symphony he felt like hearing. A clerical worker with $119 for a discount airline ticket, a Sony Walkman, and a pineapple can enjoy what Rockefeller could only dream of.

In a country of such wealth, it is no remarkable thing to claim a piece of the action for oneself. Wealth is being created all around us. If we position our money correctly, we can get our share.

ACCUMULATING SOMETHING TO INVEST

But we must have some money to begin with. The first step to investing is to amass some capital. As I explained before, the odds are excellent that you have already amassed some capital, in a savings account, life insurance policy, payroll savings plan, or elsewhere. But you might have none, and you might well not have enough.

What you must do is divert some of your income from

current consumption. Robert Louis Stevenson described one of the worthy goals of life like this: "To earn a little, to spend a little less." It is a hard prescription, but a necessary one. Ultimately, it can be very rewarding.

Giving up a little consumption now will provide you with the means for a great deal of consumption later, because of the way your investment will grow. (As we saw in Chapter 1, just $2 a week diverted from buying lottery tickets can turn into $33,349. Playing the lottery may be fun, but is it $33,349 worth of fun?) Most employable people *can* accumulate capital. But it does require the discipline of not spending everything you earn. (And it certainly requires the discipline of not using credit cards to spend money you have not yet earned.)

Many people plan on putting a certain portion of their income, say 10 percent, into savings. But that budget item is often the first thing cut when times are hard—or when winter coats go on sale in January. (One way to resist cutting it is to arrange for regular direct deposits from your checking account or paycheck into an investment plan.) You should resist all interruptions to your savings program. You should consider your commitment to save as being no less important than your commitment to make your mortgage payment or pay your telephone bill. Your future financial independence is just as important as your house or being able to call Uncle Willard in Albuquerque. I am not suggesting that you should skip mortgage payments to put the money into savings. I am saying that you should be just as reluctant to skip saving as you would be to skip a mortgage payment. Obviously, in a true emergency, savings may have to be stopped or even dipped into, but, short of emergencies, you should treat your obligations to yourself with the same respect you accord your obligations to others.

Saving money is rarely an easy task. Living on less than you earn is difficult for working people and every member of their families. Asking people to begin an investment program by reducing their current standard of living may be perceived as unfair and doomed to failure. It is like putting someone on a crash diet. Such diets do not work. The only way to take weight off—and keep it off—is to modify eating habits so that the dieter stays satisfied but is in fact eating less. If you can divert a portion of your income from consumption into investment without any problem, great. If you can explain the laudable purpose of your investment program to other members of your family and they cheerfully go along, swell. Otherwise, you might try this:

For the next twenty-four months, continue to live on your current income. You will probably receive a raise during the next year, but do not spend the extra money. Put it all into your savings program and continue to live on your pre-raise salary. This will not require any reduction in your standard of living. You are *already* living on your current salary. (Actually, to the extent that prices go up, your standard of living will decline; fortunately we are in a low-inflation period.) When you get a second raise, then start living at the level of your first raise. And carry this on indefinitely. Always live at the level of the raise before last, and put all the proceeds of your latest raise directly into your investment program. To make this plan work, you have to get through just one raise period (generally one year) without improving your standard of living. Those twelve months of sacrifice, out of the six hundred or more months of your adult life, will make all the difference in the world to you. Do it, and you will be on your way to accumulating substantial wealth. Don't do it, and you will spend your entire life haunted by vague but insistent financial worries.

People attempting to begin savings programs today have been given an extra boost by the 1986 tax cuts. The tax rates have not been so low for decades. In the future they can only go up (and I expect they will). So make hay while the sun shines. Apply your tax savings—or at least a portion of them—directly to your investment program. Take advantage of what may be a once-in-a-lifetime opportunity to keep a few extra of your own dollars.

It's fair to predict that the next two years will demonstrate conclusively whether or not you will someday achieve financial independence. If you start a savings plan, some unexpected expenses will arise. Unexpected expenses *always* arise. You will either use these inevitable unexpected expenses as an excuse to nibble away at your savings, or you will not. If you can get through two years without making excuses to dip into your savings, you will probably never make such excuses (and the money put aside during the first two years alone will grow into a substantial sum, thanks to compound interest). You will someday be financially independent. If you cannot get through two years without making such excuses, then you probably can't get through the two years after that with your savings intact either. You might as well put down this book right now and resign yourself to a lifetime of just getting by.

THE IMPORTANCE OF STARTING NOW

If you are going to begin an investment program, it is absolutely crucial that you do it soon, not just because of the dangers of procrastination, but also because of the inescapable logic of mathematics. We have already had a look at the wonders of compound interest, but we should look again. With compound interest, a sum does not increase arithmetically; it increases geometrically. That means that money does not grow at the same rate forever. The longer it is held, the faster it grows. Eventually, it grows at a truly dizzying pace.

Consider, for example, the sum of $10,000 invested at age thirty-five and held until age sixty-five. At 10 percent compound interest, that $10,000 will grow to $174,494. If that same $10,000 were invested at age twenty-five, however, it would grow by age sixty-five to $452,592. Thus, a single dollar not invested at age twenty-five represents $45 you will not have tomorrow. The investments you make when you are young will be the most effective ones you ever make. This property of compound interest also points up the real tragedy of chasing after illusive get-rich-quick schemes. It is bad enough to lose the money you invest in those schemes, but it is even worse to lose the years of relentless compounding that money could be enjoying if it had been invested prudently.

In some ways, it is relatively easy to save when you are young, because you are unlikely to have expensive family obligations. On the other hand, there are sure to be a lot of things around you would like to buy. The pain involved in not spending some of the money you earn can be eased—and this is true at any age—if you keep in mind that the money you save is not being taken from you forever. It is simply being diverted to buy something grander in the future. Do not think: "I am saving $2,000 this year that I could have used to buy an above-ground swimming pool." Think: "I am putting aside money for my future purchase of a vacation/retirement home in the mountains of North Carolina instead of buying an above-ground swimming pool."

You are not, after all, investing so that someday you can dive into a pile of money like Scrooge McDuck. (At least, you shouldn't be.) You are investing to do some very nice things for yourself—buying that new home, sending your children to college, taking a world cruise, financing a mid-life career change, making sure that you don't have to live on a Broadway IRT train when you are seventy-five years old.

You should spell out exactly what your investment objectives are. This will not only make you feel better about putting money aside. It will also guide you toward the right kinds of investments. Not every investment is appropriate for every purpose. You should therefore make clear to all involved exactly what it is you are investing for. How much money do you want? How much do you have to start with? What do you want to accumulate money for? How much time do you have to reach your goals?

When these questions have clear answers, and you are committed to creating a pool of capital by not spending all that you earn, and you have learned to treat your own savings program with the same respect you accord the telephone company, then you are ready to begin.

CHAPTER 3

SETTING GOALS— AND REACHING THEM

THE IMPORTANCE OF GOALS

Among the many investment books on the market today is one entitled *Die Rich*.

No thank you.

I mean, I have no objection to leaving a vast estate behind me when I go, but neither do I have any objection to leaving no estate behind me at all. One owes one's children love, and support during the early years of life, and enough education to prepare them to make their ways in the world. One does not owe them $500,000, payable upon the death of dear old Dad. If the money is there for them when I'm gone, that's nice. But if I have to sacrifice my own enjoyment of my own life to leave it behind, no thank you. I'll just leave them the family Bible, some photographs of myself, and my very best wishes for the future.

Now, you may feel differently. You might have a strong desire to create a family fortune. Or your financial goal might be to accumulate enough money to be the first person on your block to buy a dirigible. Or you may want to indulge in some "rich man's graffiti" by leaving your alma mater a building with your name on it. Most likely, however, you want what most people want—the comfortable feeling of financial serenity.

Whatever it may be, you should have a goal. Many people avoid setting goals for themselves, for a very simple reason. People who have goals risk failure. Whoever knows about their goals (even if it's only themselves) will know if they fail to reach them. People without goals can never fail in this way. A goal is a challenge. It is easier not to have one.

It is also foolish not to have one. If you have a reasonable financial goal, or even a slightly unreasonable one, you can achieve it. Keeping a financial target fixed in your mind will help give you the discipline you will need along the way. If you have no goal, all of your income is likely to pass through your hands as you receive it, leaving you to trust to luck for the future.

It is well worth stating your goal in very concrete terms. If your goal is to be rich, figure out what you mean by "rich." One person's luxury, after all, is another person's TV dinner. If you really think about it, you will probably decide that you don't want to be *too* rich. If you suddenly inherited $100 million, odds are that you would lose most of your friends. (They would be envious of you; you wouldn't know if they loved you for yourself; they couldn't afford to go out to dinner with you at your new favorite restaurants; your new bodyguard would probably make them nervous; etc.) And simply taking care of that much money is a full-time job. No time to go fishing if you have to keep a constant eye on the London, Zurich, and Singapore money markets, as well as your investments in Patagonia. So what's the point?

Think about it carefully, and you may conclude that your goal is to have a net worth of, say, $700,000 by the time you turn sixty-two. If you're now in your thirties or thereabouts, this may be a very realistic ambition. Specifying exactly what you're aiming at will enable you to calculate what you need to do to achieve it—how much you need to invest every year and what rate of return you need to earn on your investment. You will be able to chart your progress year by year and see when you are falling behind and when you are getting ahead.

Once you've calculated what you want and seen what it will require to get it, you may even decide to change your goal. If reaching it requires that you invest $10,000 a year and the only way you can possibly save that much money to invest is by working at a high-paying job you detest, then you probably ought to reconsider. Is it worth being miserable for the next thirty years to be happy for the twenty years after that? Could you possibly *be* happy for the twenty years after that? Maybe you should become a forest ranger after all and resign yourself to more modest means forever.

WHERE DO YOU STAND?

The first step toward reaching your goal, whatever it is, is to establish your current net worth. Businesses figure out where they stand by drawing up "balance sheets." You should do the same.

Begin by drawing a vertical line down a piece of paper.

On the left side list your assets—everything you own that is worth money. List every asset at its current market value.

Unfortunately, you cannot stop there, although some people try to. How often have you read about fabulously wealthy people who suddenly go broke? They had the house in Beverly Hills and the chalet in St. Moritz and the Ferraris and the jewels, and the next thing you know they are standing in front of some judge somewhere saying it was drugs, or liquor, or illegal inside information that led them to ruin, and would their creditors consider settling up for $5,000 and the old Chevrolet the cook used to drive?

These people had a lot of assets, yes, but they had very little net worth. That's because of what was on the *right* side of their balance sheet.

The right side is where you list your liabilities, or everything you owe (including amounts you owe on the assets listed on the left side of the balance sheet). If you own a house worth $100,000 and you owe $50,000 on the mortgage, and you have $8,000 worth of stocks, and you owe your mother-in-law $5,000, your balance sheet would look like this:

Personal Balance Sheet

ASSETS		LIABILITIES	
Cash	$ 14,000	Mortgage	$50,000
House (Market Value)	100,000	Debt to "Mom"	5,000
Stocks	8,000	Car Loan	6,000
Personal Assets (jewelry, paintings, etc.)	4,000	Total Liabilities	$61,000
Total Assets	$126,000	Total Assets	126,000
		Total Liabilities	61,000
		DIFFERENCE = NET WORTH	$65,000

The total value of all your assets minus the total of all your liabilities is your net worth. In this case, your net worth is $65,000.

THE PERILS OF "POCKET ACCOUNTING"

Most balance sheets are in fact a good deal more complicated than this. Carefully examined, balance sheets can show you not only how much you have but also whether what you have is well distributed. It is generally advisable to have your assets diversified among several different types of investments. Many people, however, do not, often as a result of what I call "pocket accounting." Over here they've stashed some money away for the kids' college education. Over there they've set up a retirement fund. They've started a special savings account for next year's vacation. And they just bought a life insurance policy to pay for their funeral.

This is not the best way to organize your money.

Dividing up your funds in this multi-pocketed fashion may distract you from the search for the most profitable ways to invest those funds. Do you remember bank-sponsored Christmas Clubs? Twenty or thirty years ago, they were very popular. People were encouraged to prepare for their holiday gift-buying by depositing some small amount in a special bank account every week. Just think, the bank advertisements crowed, you put in a mere ten dollars a week for fifty weeks, and at the end of the year you'll have *five hundred dollars*. That is, in fact, exactly what many banks paid back to their Christmas Club depositors—just five hundred dollars, *with no interest*. The depositors' focus on the specific objective of the savings program blinded them to its severe limitations.

Most people today are too sophisticated to dream of enrolling in a no-interest Christmas Club, yet, by neglecting to think about their assets as a unified whole, they may still be failing to maximize their investment profits. Some investments pay more than others, and those are the investments your money should be in, regardless of how convenient it may seem to allocate your money here and there for specific purposes. Putting $5 a week in the cookie jar may indeed help you save up for a new refrigerator, but it shouldn't be asking too much of yourself to have the discipline to contribute your refrigerator money to an investment program where it will accumulate more than chocolate chip crumbs. You can still take money out to buy a refrigerator when its time comes.

To see how pocket accounting may cause a family's funds to be improperly diversified, consider a couple whose primary assets are company pension plans that will pay them $2,000 a month for life after they retire. In the meantime, they maintain bank accounts in their children's names that they set up years before to provide for their kids' college educations. Finally, both husband and wife have $100,000 life insurance policies, to help the surviving spouse adjust to becoming head of a single-income family.

This couple's assets are not negligible, but they are very badly distributed. Every one of their investments has an upper growth limit. Their $2,000-a-month pensions may seem adequate today, but by retirement time inflation is likely to have substantially reduced their value. The children's bank accounts, even if they are earning 8 percent in the form of certificates of deposit, will forever pay that fixed interest rate and nothing more. A $100,000 insurance policy will never be worth more than $100,000, and that, like the fixed pensions, may be decimated by inflation. This couple should have a portion of their assets in stocks or real estate—investments that are riskier than the ones they have but that have historically kept pace with inflation. Pocket accounting has caused this couple to put all their eggs in a limited-growth basket.

Another common example of those with poorly diversified assets are people who are house-rich. Think of a couple who have raised a family in a three-bedroom house they have owned for twenty years. Now the kids are gone, and the couple is alone. Over the years, their house has appreciated in value; it is now worth $300,000. All they owe on the mortgage is $25,000. Their other assets are $25,000 in cash, stocks, and bonds. This couple may never have thought about it this way, but more than 90 percent of their assets are in a single real estate investment—their house. They may love the house dearly and want to stay in it come hell or high water (or at least until the dog dies). Or, once they realize the situation they are in, they might be perfectly happy to sell the house, buy a small condominium, and put the rest of the money into a well-diversified investment program.

THINKING ABOUT RETIREMENT

But what about retirement? Since providing for a comfortable retirement is such an important and all-encompassing goal, doesn't it make sense to indulge in some pocket accounting for that?

The answer is yes, and no.

It certainly makes sense to take advantage of the excellent investment opportunities that have been created by the federal government and many private employers with retirement in mind. Many of these opportunities are "tax-advantaged." That is, they provide a legal way to avoid—or, at least, delay—paying income tax on some current income. Well-to-do taxpayers have been taking advantage of "tax shelters" for years. (Sometimes they have saved themselves large sums of money; sometimes they have done less well than they expected.) But tax-advantaged investments are no longer the exclusive preserve of the well-to-do. Today they exist for everybody. You should know about them, and you should take advantage of them.

The IRA Lives

The best-known tax-advantaged investment is the Individual Retirement Account (IRA). Congress created IRAs in 1974 for individuals who had no employer's pension plan. In 1981 the law was changed so that everybody, even those covered by pension plans, could have IRAs. Millions of Americans of all income levels realized that the IRA was a great deal. By 1986, 40 million people had put $250 billion into IRAs, and IRAs were still growing at a rapid rate.

Then came the tax reform bill, which put some limitations on IRAs. This created a widespread misconception that IRAs were dead, or as good as dead. But that simply isn't true. For a substantial proportion of working Americans (those who are not covered by employer-sponsored retirement plans, or those who are covered by such plans but earn less than a certain amount), IRAs are still as good a deal as they ever were. For everybody else, IRAs now offer reduced but still valuable tax savings that, in the long run, can be worth tens or even hundreds of thousands of dollars.

To understand the benefits of IRAs, consider the investment programs of three prototypical individuals, Ira X. Ample and his sisters Shirley and Betty. Under the new law, Ira and Shirley are still eligible for all the benefits of the pre-1986 IRA. Ira is eligible because he is self-employed and thus not covered by any employee retirement plan. Shirley has a job and is part of a company pension plan, but she is eligible for full IRA benefits anyway because she earns less than $25,000 a year.[1] Betty is not eligible for an original-style IRA, because she is covered by a company retirement plan and she makes more than $35,000 a year, but she is still eligible for the most valuable IRA benefit.

Both Ira and Betty open IRA accounts; Shirley doesn't bother. Ira and Betty each deposit $2,000 into their accounts. Ira—but not Betty—is allowed to deduct that $2,000 from his current-year taxable income. This is the difference between old-style and new-style IRAs. This is the benefit that people who are covered by employee retirement plans and earn over a certain amount are no longer eligible for.

But Ira is still eligible, so he gets an immediate and welcome cut in his tax bill. Ira's income is $30,000, which means his federal income tax is $4,694. But, because Ira put $2,000 of his income into an IRA, he only has to pay taxes on $28,000, for a federal tax bill of $4,134, and an immediate savings of $560.

Taxes *are* payable on that $2,000, but not until the money is withdrawn from the IRA. The program is designed so that most IRA funds will be withdrawn by individuals after they retire, when their incomes (and thus their tax rates) will presumably be lower. Consider what might happen in Ira X. Ample's case. Some years after

[1]People covered by company-sponsored retirement plans are eligible for all IRA benefits if they are single and earn less than $25,000 a year, or if they are married and their joint income is less than $40,000. Single people who earn between $25,000 and $35,000 a year and married people whose joint incomes are between $40,000 and $50,000 are partially eligible for original-style IRA benefits.

putting his first $2,000 into an IRA, he retires and takes it
out. As a retiree, his taxable income has declined to $15,000
(including that $2,000 he withdraws from his IRA). He will
now pay $300 in federal income tax on that $2,000. That is
$260 less that he would have had to pay on it years before
had he not "sheltered" that money in his IRA.

Saving that $260 is nice, but it is the *least* important
advantage of an IRA. Every year that Ira's $2,000 sits in
his IRA, it earns some return. It might well be invested in
securities earning 10 percent.[2] We have already seen how
compound interest makes even modest investments grow
to enormous sums if enough time is allowed to elapse.
Unfortunately, in most investments income tax must be
paid on each year's interest income. This reduces the
effectiveness of compound interest by reducing the amount
of money that is left to compound. The greatest advantage
of IRAs, and the aspect of IRAs that is still available to
Betty as well as Ira—it is, in fact, available to *everybody*—is
that the income they produce is not taxed until it is
withdrawn years later. In the meantime, your money is
left to compound tax-free.

Let's see what that means.

Suppose Ira, Betty and Shirley each have $2,000 to
invest. All of them are in the 28 percent tax bracket. All of
them invest their money in securities paying 10 percent
interest. Ira and Betty put their money into IRAs; Shirley
does not.

After one year, the siblings will have earned interest of

---

[2]An IRA is not in itself an investment. IRA funds must be invested in
stocks, bonds, certificates of deposit, or other securities to start earning
money. In theory, you could put your IRA money into a bank account
earning 0 percent interest, although that would be idiotic. I will deal
with the specific investments available to IRA holders, and everybody
else, beginning in Chapter 5.

$200 apiece on their money. Shirley's $200 is immediately taxed. She gets to keep $144 of it. Ira's and Betty's $200, inside their IRAs, is not taxed. So, as the second year begins, Ira and Betty each have $2,200, while Shirley has only $2,144. Another year goes by, and the siblings have earned another 10 percent on their money. Shirley's interest is taxed again; Ira's and Betty's is not. Ira and Betty now have $2,420; Shirley has $2,298.

Many more years go by, and compound interest begins to work its magic. After twenty years, Shirley's original investment has grown to $8,034. After thirty years, she has $16,102. After forty years, she has $32,272.

Not bad, but take a look at Ira and Betty. After twenty years they each have $13,455. After thirty years they each have $34,898. After forty years they each have $90,519. (This is from a single investment of $2,000, mind you.) After forty years, because their interest has not been taxed, Ira's and Betty's accounts are each more than two times greater than that of their sister. (It is true that Ira and Betty must, at last, pay income tax on their accumulated earnings as they withdraw them, but what they have gained from tax-free compounding over the years will far outweigh their belated tax burden.)

If Ira puts $2,000 into his IRA every year, instead of just once, after forty years he will have $973,704. If Shirley also saves $2,000 to invest every year, and puts the $1,440 that is left to her after taxes into her non-IRA program, after forty years she will have $324,512. Betty will come out somewhere in between her siblings in a program like this. Like Shirley, her annual contributions are not tax-deductible. If she saves $2,000 to invest, she must pay $560 in taxes on it first. But, unlike Shirley, Betty's investment compounds tax-free. Thus her account shows a balance of $701,067 after forty years. This puts Betty $376,555 ahead of Shirley, all because Betty opened an IRA—which some people say isn't worth doing anymore![3]

IRAs do have some restrictions that you should be aware of before you start one. If you have an old-style IRA—one to which your contributions are tax-deductible—you may not withdraw any money from the account before you reach the age of 59½ without paying a 10 percent penalty on top of the income tax due. IRAs were designed with retirement in mind, not just to let anyone who feels like it defer taxes to some future year of his or her choice. Therefore the penalty. (If your IRA is of the nondeductible variety, however, you may freely withdraw your contributions at any time, since you have already paid income tax on them.)[4]

Other Retirement Plans

So IRAs are far from dead. And they are not the only valuable tax-advantaged investments now available to all taxpayers. Annuities, which are created by insurance companies and marketed by insurance companies and brokers, have become very popular of late because they offer the same big benefit of IRAs—tax-deferred compounding—and some additional advantages. (There is more on annuities in Chapter 5.)

---

[3]All of these examples assume that the siblings always earn 10 percent on their investments and that tax rates never change. If these assumptions prove false, actual results will differ. But Ira will always come out ahead of his sisters, with Betty in second place and Shirley far behind.

[4]With either kind of IRA, you can withdraw your money for a little while without paying a penalty. IRA holders are allowed to "roll over" their money from one IRA to another once a year. You can take all your money out of your current IRA and do whatever you want with it for as many as 60 days, as long as the money is then deposited in another IRA. This is a great way to take advantage of a hot tip on a speculative new stock, although, needless to say, it would not be prudent to do so.

For some taxpayers, there are still other tax-advantaged opportunities available. The government allows self-employed individuals to establish Keogh plans, which work like IRAs but permit those who qualify to make tax-deferred deposits of up to 20 percent of their incomes (to a maximum of $30,000) every year. Self-employed people can actually benefit doubly. They may have both Keogh plans *and* IRAs.

Many large corporations offer their employees savings programs that are better yet. Known as 401(k) plans (after the section of the tax code that makes them possible), the programs allow employees to make tax-deferred contributions, often in amounts greater than the $2,000 maximum allowed in an IRA. Accumulated 401(k) funds may be borrowed against, while IRA funds may not. The best thing about 401(k) plans, however, is that many employers match part or all of their employees' contributions, giving their employees an immediate guaranteed profit. If your employer offers such a plan, jump in. You can't go wrong taking someone else's money.

EIGHT STEPS TO INVESTMENT SUCCESS

All of these plans—IRAs, Keoghs, 401(k)s, annuities— are geared to retirement, but you should not succumb to pocket accounting and think of them in isolation from the rest of your investments. They should constitute part, but not all, of your retirement planning, just as they constitute part, but not all, of your investment program. Whatever types of investments you have selected for your IRA, you should take care that they balance your non-IRA investments for proper diversification. Your "retirement funds" are not entities in themselves; they are cohesive parts of the overall plan by which you are going to achieve financial serenity.

Before I get into the specifics of selecting and maintaining investments, let's quickly review the outline of what you will need to do:

1. Convert income dollars to capital dollars.

This is just another way of saying that you must spend less than you earn. Capital (as in capitalism) is required to begin any kind of investment program. Once you have amassed some capital by saving, then your money can begin to make money for you. No capital, no investment income.

2. If it's not already too late, start while you're young.

As we have seen, the phenomenon of compound interest delivers its most fantastic rewards to those who put their money to work for the longest time. At 10 percent compound interest, a single dollar invested at age thirty-five will grow to $17 by age sixty-five. That same dollar, invested at age twenty-five, would grow to $45 by age sixty-five. Whatever age you are, your investment fund will grow larger if you begin it today instead of a week from Tuesday. You should start as soon as you finish this book. Better yet, as soon as you finish this chapter.

3. Have a simple plan.

Calculate where you are and where you want to go. Understand exactly how much your money must grow each year to enable you to reach your goal.

4. Be realistic.

Make sure you understand and accept, both intellectually and *emotionally*, that it will not be possible for you to find $10 stocks that go to $15 in six months. Ten-dollar stocks that go up between fifty cents and one dollar in a year while paying an annual dividend of between fifty cents and one dollar (or other investments that earn equivalent returns) are all you can realistically hope to find, but they will do quite nicely for you. Given enough time, they will make you a small fortune.

5. Be patient and disciplined.

It will take many years of compounding for your investments to grow. Do not be tempted to take risky shortcuts because you are bored. Do not let greed cause you to divert your money into get-rich-quick "sure things." Remember that there is no Santa Claus. If a cyclical market downturn sends your investments in the wrong direction, do not panic and sell out. If your investments have been successful for a number of years, do not become arrogant in the belief that you have figured out the financial world and attempt to do something "clever." Stick to your plan.

6. Avoid flat years.

Your plan will require that your investments grow by a certain percentage every year. If your goal is 10 percent annual growth, and one year you pursue some wild goose and don't make a cent, then the following year your money must grow by 20 percent to get back on course. (Actually, it would have to grow by 21 percent, because the 10 percent growth you missed the previous year would itself have contributed 1 percent growth via compounding.) Earning your normal investment goal every year is likely to be difficult enough. Doubling it because you missed a year is likely to be impossible.

7. Avoid major life disruptions.

This is easier said than done, but that makes it no less important. Your financial plan is apt to be fatally derailed if, at the age of fifty, you decide to chuck your spouse in favor of the swimming pool attendant at the country club. Likewise, your plan is likely to go awry if you become a drunk, or a cocaine addict, or become caught up in a religious fervor and donate all your worldly goods to the Guru Maharaj Ji. Try to be stable.

8. Leave it to the power of compound interest to generate your wealth.

Remember that you are investing for the long term. Remember that you are *investing*, not trading pieces of paper for a profit.

What you are attempting to do is affiliate your money with enterprises that are creating wealth. If you can do that, you don't need to chase after short-term speculative profits.

And you *can* do that. In America, it is not difficult to find wealth-creating enterprises. Consider, for example, the activities of one group of 540,000 Americans. Every weekday morning, at widely scattered locations all over the country, these people get up and scowl at their alarm clocks. They eat some cornflakes or chocolate donuts and haul themselves out to their cars or bus stops. After a while they arrive at offices or factories. In the storage yards of the factories are heaps of steel, rubber, glass, plastic, and other supplies. The offices are filled with telephones and paper.

As the day progresses, some of these people spend their time sweeping floors. Some of them operate blast furnaces. Some of them weld things to other things. Some of them draw things. Some of them fly off to sales meetings and buy other people martinis. Some of them don't seem to be doing much of anything at all.

Nevertheless, by the end of the day, a minor miracle has occurred. More than 25,000 brand-new automobiles, *which did not exist that morning*, have been created. An organization called General Motors has so effectively marshaled together ideas, supplies, and the efforts of 540,000 people that it has been able to produce 25,000 Chevrolets, Buicks, Oldsmobiles, Pontiacs, and Cadillacs where, before, there were only piles of iron ore and other raw materials.

This is a successful business enterprise creating wealth. Such an enterprise utilizes its assets to create new assets. And this is something that, historically, American business has been very good at. Over the modern history of the American economy, through booms and recessions, counting good companies and bad ones, large ones and small, the average rate of growth of American corporations has been about 10 percent. This has been triple the average rate of inflation. Real profits have been made. Real wealth has been created.

The rest of the world has taken notice of this success. Today even China and other Communist countries are paying this wealth-creating process the ultimate compliment; they are beginning to imitate it. Unlike the residents of Beijing, you don't have to settle for an imitation. You can associate your capital with American business and reap the benefits.

CHAPTER 4

SEEKING HELP

THE FALLIBLE EXPERTS

A few years ago, the New York *Daily News* asked one of my colleagues to participate in something called the "Battle of the Brokers." Each contestant was given a hypothetical $30,000 to invest any way he wished. Whoever had made the most money after two months was the winner.

My colleague won. He had an idea that interest rates were about to decline, and he invested his stake in securities that would go up if they did. They did—and the value of his securities increased 26 percent in just two months.

Three other investment professionals who took part in the competition did not fare so well. All three are well respected and have had years of experience on Wall Street. All three actually *lost* money during the test.

Only one other entry showed a profit. That was the

Daily News Dart Fund, so named because it was a portfolio of stocks selected by *Daily News* reporters throwing
darts at a stock table pinned to the office wall. Ten darts
were thrown, and the ten stocks they landed on were
purchased. The Dart Fund finished the contest in a respectable second place. It appreciated 3.4 percent in two
months, which is equivalent to annual growth of more
than 20 percent.

Does this mean that you should throw away this book
and buy a package of darts? Probably not. A dart can't tell
you about the tax advantages of an IRA. (And, while you
may be entitled to deduct the cost of this book on your
income tax return as a tax-preparation expense, it would
be harder to convince the IRS to let you write off the
darts.)

What the success of the Dart Fund should tell you is
that nobody knows for certain what the market is going to
do, especially over the short term (and two months is
definitely short term). If you're looking for quick profits,
you probably would do just as well to throw a dart as
consult an expert.

But wait a minute, you say, aren't there a number of
renowned authorities who have made fortunes for investors (and themselves) by telling people what to buy and
what to sell, week by week and month by month?

Let me answer that question by introducing you to ten
thousand monkeys. Some of the monkeys are smart (for
monkeys), and some are as thick as bricks. They're all
sitting in one big room, and you go in there and stand up
in front of them early one morning, and you say, "Attention, monkeys! Please tell me, is the market going to go up
or down today?"

The monkeys look at you, and they don't have the
slightest idea what you're talking about, so you decide to

make things easy for them. "Okay, monkeys," you say, "if you think the market is going to go up today, the next time you scratch your head use your right hand to do it. If you think the market will go down, use your left hand."

The monkeys go about their business, and you keep an eye on them until all ten thousand have scratched. Assuming there's no such thing as a right-handed monkey (if there is, this whole story is wrong, but you get the idea), about half of them will scratch with their right hands and the other half will scratch with their left hands. You make a list of who scratched with which hand and then go off to work. At the end of the day, you check to see how the market did and then get rid of all the monkeys who made the wrong prediction. If the market went down, you send all those who scratched with their right hands packing, and vice versa.

The next morning, you stand in front of the 5,000 remaining monkeys and ask for another prediction. At the end of the day, 2,500 will be winners again. After three days, 1,250 will have been right every time. After four days, 625 will still be on a perfect streak. And on it will go. After thirteen days, there will be 1 monkey who has been correct every single morning, 1 monkey whose predictions would have made you a fortune if you had bought and sold on his advice.

What do you think the odds are that that monkey will be right again on day fourteen? Will you bet money on it?

Someday you may encounter an investment advisor who has been right thirteen times in a row. He or she may be a person of unusual brilliance who is going to be right forevermore. Or he or she may only have been lucky. There are, after all, more than ten thousand investment advisors at large in the land. The laws of probability apply to them just as they do to monkeys.

This does not mean, however, that you should go it alone in the financial world, even if you are confident that you know as much about investing as a monkey. I know more—I have been in the investment business for forty years—and *I* employ the services of a stockbroker, because his time is devoted, day after day, to following the securities markets, while I am often occupied with other matters.

If you are not in the investment business yourself, you will need to consult with a broker to execute even those decisions you make on your own. Whether you're opening an IRA, buying a bond, or selling a rental property, you cannot transact your business at the zoo.

More importantly, the right kind of advice can give you an edge over those random monkeys. Half of those creatures fell on their faces every time out, and so will you if you operate by your own guesswork. The advice you can get from an investment professional will not always be correct, but if it is correct just 55 percent of the time, over the years you will be significantly better off with it than without it. The key to achieving this modest but important advantage over even odds is to avoid asking questions that cannot be answered—what is the market going to do tomorrow?—and to understand the limitations of all predictions.

THE UNPREDICTABLE MARKET

Suppose, to begin, that you try to do it yourself. You take to studying the financial pages of your local newspaper, and you subscribe to *The Wall Street Journal*, *Fortune*, and *Forbes*. You tune in to *Wall Street Week*, the *Nightly*

Business Report, and the Financial News Network. You read books about the Federal Reserve System and syndicated columns about the money supply. Your spouse wants to know why you mention Alan Greenspan's name in your sleep.

Where does it all get you?

You will become an educated person with an excellent understanding of the forces at work in the economic world around you. You will gain insights into the relationships between interest rates, inflation, and the prices of various investments. You will be able to avoid making some stupid mistakes, and spitting into the wind. You may even become a happier and a more confident person.

You will *not* know what is going to happen to the price of anything tomorrow.

Basically, that's because other people know how to read too. By the time you pick up the morning *Wall Street Journal* and read that United Sprockets has just been awarded a $10 billion government contract, a couple of million other people already know about it. Some of them got their paper before you did. Some of them saw the news on the financial wire the day before. Most significantly, a lot of them *expected* this to happen. They knew that the Defense Department was running short of sprockets. They knew that United Sprockets was a contender for the contract.

This is why stocks often *fall* when good news is announced. The good news has been anticipated and was *already* built into the price of the stock. In most cases, this does not mean that "insiders," such as corporate officials and their friends, have been trading illegally on the basis of inside information. This does happen sometimes, as the recent series of prosecutions by the Securities and Exchange Commission makes clear. Usually, however, the prospects of individual companies are foreseen, completely legally, by people whose job it is to keep track of developments in various industries. Such people don't have to wait to read a newspaper article to find out what is going on. They can talk to the same people the reporter talks to.

Economists have a theory to explain why you cannot predict which way stock prices will move. (It would be nicer if they had a theory that *would* predict which way prices will move; a theory explaining why that is impossible seems like a poor consolation prize to me.) They call it the "efficient market theory." It says that in an efficient market—and the stock market is one—the significance of all new information is quickly apparent to market participants and is immediately reflected in prices. The speed with which such information affects prices may seem miraculous. (The classic economics textbook by Paul Samuelson and William Nordhaus cites a study that found that you could profit from stock-related news only if you bought or sold the stock within thirty seconds after the news was first made public.) But there is nothing magical about it. It merely results from the fact that thousands of very smart and diligent people are constantly looking out for information that will affect stock prices, and some of them inevitably are finding it and acting on it. Of course, stock prices will still be driven up and down by totally unexpected news, like a gas leak that sends United Sprocket's main factory up in flames. But it's awfully hard to profit from that kind of news. If it's unanticipated, you cannot anticipate it. It's certainly too late to act by the time you see the story in the next day's newspaper.

Despite all this, there is no shortage of people prepared to tell you exactly what the market is going to do in the near future—for a price. Expensive newsletters published by stock market seers can be yours if you want them (and another newsletter, *The Hulbert Financial Digest*, does nothing but keep track of the success or failure of the recommendations of sixty other newsletters). Some of these seers have been right several times in a row. (Some of them have been right because their prophecies are self-fulfilling. They have so many followers that, when they recommend a stock, their own followers' purchases alone drive the price up—at least temporarily.) But always remember that past success does not mean that tomorrow morning's prediction will be accurate. Maybe the monkey's luck has run out.

The soundest investment advice has nothing to do with what is going to happen to the market tomorrow. It deals instead with the fundamental underlying value of securities you are considering purchasing, and it deals with the way any suggested investment suits your own particular situation and goals. There are people qualified to give you this kind of advice. You would be wise to employ their expertise.

SELECTING A BROKER

Investment advice is available at many outlets nowadays. While you once could buy insurance only from an insurance agent, real estate only from a real estate broker, and stocks only from a stockbroker, and you automatically kept your ready cash in a bank, the lines between those institutions have broken down in the current atmosphere of deregulation. Today banks have cooperative arrangements with firms that sell stocks and life insurance, and many Wall Street brokerage firms sell everything from stocks to money market funds (that you can write checks on) to shares in real estate limited partnerships.

This is all to your benefit, since a "stockbroker" who has much more than stocks to sell will be able to select freely from among his or her many financial products to find the ones that suit you best. Brokers are, of course, paid on a commission basis, so it is in their interest to sell you something. But a broker who has many different investment vehicles to offer will earn a commission no matter what you buy; there will generally be no incentive to steer you toward something unsuitable. Brokers are sometimes encouraged to "push" certain investments, including securities the brokerage firm may be selling from its own inventory account, but an honest broker will not take advantage of you. And *any* broker will realize that he or she is better off in the long run to have satisfied, not aggrieved, clients. The best source of new accounts is referrals from happy customers.

There is no fixed prescription for finding the broker that is right for you. It is largely a matter of chemistry. An important part of your relationship with a broker will be how you feel about him or her, so choosing a broker involves aspects of personality that cannot be quantified. (How did you choose your doctor? Your veterinarian? Your auto mechanic?) You might begin by asking friends for recommendations. Or you can simply march into a brokerage office and ask them what they can do for you.

There is, by the way, no reason to feel shy about walking unannounced into a broker's office because you're afraid you don't have enough money to invest or don't know enough to ask the right questions. Most brokers today (unlike in years past) will be glad to see you, even if your means are modest. A small client today might become a major client tomorrow. And, even if you're not in a position to buy any stock right now, they might be able to help you (and themselves) by opening an IRA for you, or putting your cash into a money market account, or starting you off with small monthly investments in a mutual fund. You've surely noticed all those ads on television with bulls running through the streets and earnest spokespersons talking about the advantages of this broker or that one. Businesses don't spend millions of dollars putting commercials like that on during *Dallas* or Wimbledon because they *don't* want people to drop by.

When you first enter a brokerage office, you might ask to speak to the manager. This person sets the tone for the place, so his or her attitude and answers to your questions will give you a quick idea if you have knocked on the right door. If the manager is not available, you may be handed over to whoever is taking "walk-ins" that day. Whomever you meet, feel free to talk for a while. And feel equally free to say good-bye.

You should talk to prospective brokers as if you were interviewing them for a job—which you are. It is the job of your personal investment advisor. This is, needless to say, an important position, so you should take care whom you engage.

Beware, first of all, of any broker who promises you too much. He or she should talk at least as much about the problems of investing as about its rewards. He or she should not imply that the process of accumulating capital will be quick or easy. He or she should not have definite answers to your questions (but *should* have strong opinions). If a broker implies that he or she can spot $10 stocks that will go to $15 in six months, or that he or she can substantially increase the value of your holdings by frequent trading in and out of various securities, run, do not walk, to the next candidate.

You want a broker who wants to know a lot about *you*—how much you earn, how much you save, what your tax status is, what your investment goals are, how much time you have to achieve them, how much risk you can afford to take, how much risk you feel comfortable taking.

You want a broker who will make a commitment to devise a well-diversified investment program to help you meet your goals and who will monitor your investments after you have purchased them, reviewing them periodically for continued suitability, instead of selling you something and disappearing from your life forever.

You want a broker who will provide *leadership* for you as you move toward your goals, who will guide your actions, who will restrain you when your investments are plummeting and you want to sell out in a panic, and restrain you again when your investments are soaring and you decide you have figured out the secrets of Wall Street. You should not be embarrassed to accept the leadership of another person in an area as personal as your own finances. It is simply good management to rely on the specialized knowledge of others in fields where you yourself are an amateur. Successful business executives do it all the time. You must be comfortable, however, with your broker's style of leadership. This is a matter of taste. One person's inspiring guide is another person's strutting Bonaparte. Choose as you will.

You want a broker, finally, who will help you develop realistic expectations for the progress of your investment program and who will help you establish yardsticks to measure whether those expectations are being met. You will not find, nor should you expect to find, a financial miracle worker. Those few brokers who are true geniuses have been promoted to executive positions, or they have developed very lucrative careers handling the accounts of very rich people and now spend much of their time improving their golf game in the Hamptons. They will not be saying hello to drop-in customers at the brokerage office in the shopping mall.

But this is no reason to despair. All you want—all you need—is a broker who will do a good, honest, average job of handling your affairs. Remember, the *average* annual appreciation of stocks in all American corporations during this century has been about 10 percent. A broker who can get you that return year after year will be doing a very nice job of leading you toward your financial goals. And not every broker will be able to get that return for you. Half of all investments, after all, turn out by definition to be below average.

The difficulty of achieving average returns has been dramatically demonstrated in recent years by the performance of the professional money managers who handle the accounts of huge pension funds and other multi-million-dollar clients. Between 1983 and 1987, two thirds of all professional money managers failed to equal the performance of the Standard & Poor 500-Stock Index (a measure that is more representative of market movement than the better-known Dow Jones Industrial Average, which tracks only thirty stocks). Some professionals have given up trying to outperform the averages; they simply invest their clients' money in portfolios consisting of every single stock used to compile the averages. By this cop-out, they guarantee that their performance will always be exactly "average," never above, but, more important, never embarrassingly below. (This timid technique is known as the "index fund" approach.)

So don't look down your nose at average performance. If you find a broker who can help you do just a little bit *better* than average, then you will be sitting pretty indeed. This is where you may take advantage of the brokerage firm's research department. That department will be made up of analysts who devote all their time to investigating the outlook for various investment possibilities. They are awash in data. Sometimes, in fact, they appear to be operating on the belief that if data are tortured sufficiently they will confess. In recent years researchers have discovered, for example, that there is a startling correlation between the movement of the stock market and the winner of the Super Bowl. Every year between 1967 and 1987 that the Super Bowl was won by a team with its roots in the original National Football League, the stock market went up. Every year the game was won by a team from the old American Football League, the market went down. (The sole exception was 1970, when the Kansas City Chiefs won the game and the Standard & Poor 500 went up a piddling .1 percent. Would that all forecasters' errors were off by such a small margin!)

Correlations have also been discovered between the lengths of women's skirts and the stock market (rising hemlines signal rising stock prices) and between major league baseball batting averages and the stock market. (If the overall average in the majors goes down from the previous year, the market often goes up, and vice versa. Analysts have suggested that batters may not be inclined to bust a gut squeezing out a hit when they are making money in the stock market without even leaving the dugout.)

This is, of course, not the kind of research data you should rely on. (It is, in fact, the kind of thing stock market analysts do for fun.) Research departments prepare careful and lengthy analyses of publicly-held corporations, which your broker will make available to you. These analyses often offer solid indications of the long-term performance of the stocks in question, but you should not be overly confident that highly rated stocks will go up any time soon. After all, somebody else's research department may have reached the same conclusion last week and already driven up the price of the stock.

Probably the most valuable service a research department can provide you is to help you avoid losers. While the researchers are uncovering well-managed companies with bright futures, they will also be coming across poorly managed turkeys. If your investments are well diversified, the growth of your portfolio will tend to approximate the average. If you can avoid just one or two losers, your portfolio will grow a little bit better than average, and that will be very nice.

Your portfolio would also grow a little bit better if you didn't have to pay commissions to your broker, but commissions are a fact of life. Compared to commissions on real estate and other valuable assets, stock brokerage commissions are quite low. Nevertheless, those who want them lower still have been attracted in recent years to "discount brokers," who charge 30 to 70 percent less than traditional brokers. (Discount brokers often have a minimum commission, however, which wipes out any discount on small trades.) Discount brokers are cheaper than traditional brokers because they do not provide the services of traditional brokers. You call them up and tell them what you want to buy. They buy it for you and send you the bill. End of transaction. End of relationship.

Not surprisingly, it is sophisticated investors who can benefit the most from discount brokers. These are people who have the confidence, time, and experience to make their own investment decisions. "Our customer profile," the founder of the nation's largest discount broker told *The New York Times*, "shows that 57 percent have been in the market for ten years, and 60 percent spend five hours a week on their portfolios."

Most investors, including all beginners, will be a lot

more comfortable dealing with a full-service broker, who will provide them with research materials, conversation, suggestions, follow-up monitoring of their investments, and, yes, a little psychological hand-holding.

THE BROKER-CLIENT RELATIONSHIP

A well-established and very successful broker I know tells this story of how he was approached by his best friend when he was first starting out in the business:

"My friend had a small amount of money to invest, about $2,000, which was just about what I had in my own portfolio. He asked me if I wanted to play with his account. I said I did not want to 'play' with it. I was very serious about investing. I knew that if we 'played' with it we would lose it. And I didn't want to be the one he associated with losing his money.

"I suggested instead that we do some things with the money that would be extremely dull. And he got mad and said, 'The hell with you. I'll go someplace else.' And he did.

"About a year later, he called me and asked if I would help out his mother, who was recently widowed. She had a small nest egg that she couldn't afford to 'play' with. He asked me how my own account was doing. I told him, 'Well, I've still got the same positions I had a year ago. How's your account doing?' He told me the broker he'd gone to had had a lot of bright ideas and had had him in and out of quite a few stocks over the year. When all was said and done, my friend had had a lot of adventures, and he'd paid a lot of commissions—and his portfolio was worth about $1,500. He brought the money to me, and we started a very dull process of slow, long-term growth."

This broker had been wise enough not to take on his friend as a client at a time when their relationship clearly would have been a failure. Only when they saw eye to eye on investment philosophy could they begin to work together.

Your relationship with your broker is likely to play a significant role in your life. A successful broker-client relationship may last for many years and be profitable for all involved. An unsuccessful one will make everyone miserable. To try to make yours work, you should be sure that your broker and you share the same goals, and you should understand what you can expect from your broker, and what you cannot.

One thing that you should get from your broker is an investment education. Your broker should be willing to explain to you exactly why he or she is recommending a particular investment, what he or she expects to happen to that investment, and by when. If your broker expects the investment to achieve its growth over a long time-frame (as he or she generally should), explaining this to you should help relieve you of worry about the "noise" of short-term up-and-down market movements. If the investment fails to perform as expected when its time has come, your broker should discuss with you why this occurred, as you formulate together a new plan of action.

All of this should not only be educational. It should also be *fun*. If you are like most people, you will enjoy participating in the investment process—discussing your investments with your broker, charting their progress, cheering them on.

You must always keep in mind, however, that you are not your broker's only client. Your broker may indeed enjoy chatting with you. He or she should certainly be dedicated to giving you the best possible advice in a timely fashion. But he or she is likely to be equally dedicated to earning a decent living. Brokers are paid according to how much they sell. They sell by spending their time talking to people. So their time is valuable. If your broker breaks off conversations with you when you shift the topic from investments to the Red Sox, don't be insulted. (If your broker has plenty of time to discuss the Red Sox with you, *then* you should begin to worry. Why doesn't he or she have anything better to do?) If you demand a large portion of your broker's time, you must expect to pay for it. Your broker will certainly expect you to.

By limiting your demands on your broker's time, you limit any temptation for him or her to sell you something you don't need. While most brokers are honest, there have been some notorious cases of "churned" accounts, where brokers have bought and sold for their clients incessantly, generating losses for the clients and huge commissions for the brokers. The basic investment philosophy of this book is that you should buy and sell very sparingly (more on this in Chapter 6). If you engage a broker who shares that philosophy, and you do not call him or her three times a day to kibitz, you should never have cause to suspect your broker of "churning."

What kind of client does a broker like best? My broker-friend describes his own all-time favorite:

"He would call me and say, 'Good morning. What can you do for me today that will improve my account?' That really opened the door for me. Often, I could answer his question by saying, 'The best thing to do today is nothing.' And he would say, 'Thank you. Good-bye.' But sometimes the best thing I could do for him was to reverse my previous advice and sell something we had recently bought.

He didn't make that hard for me to do. He didn't rehash all my past mistakes. He never looked back."

My friend happens to be an excellent broker, so he didn't find himself reversing his previous advice very often. While it is important to be flexible and not set your investment portfolio in stone, it is equally important not to set it in quicksand. If you find that your broker is constantly backtracking on previous advice and selling today what you bought last week, or even last year, you should reconsider your affiliation. The best investments are bought and held for the long haul. If your broker fights you on this, you have the wrong broker. If you cannot accept this yourself and are constantly tempted to go for a quick killing, it will be easy to find a broker who will oblige you. We all get the brokers we deserve.

CHAPTER 5

YOUR INVESTMENT PROGRAM—BASIC CHOICES

THE ELUSIVE PERFECT INVESTMENT

Just so you'll know it in case you ever run across it, this is what the perfect investment would look like:

1. It pays a guaranteed high rate of return, at least double the current rate of inflation. Assuming inflation continues to be less than 5 percent, we'll settle for 10 percent here.

2. Your principal (the money you have invested) is absolutely safe. It is guaranteed by the United States government or, better yet, by the combined resources of NATO, OPEC, Superman, and Michael Jackson.

3. The potential for growth is excellent. While paying you 10 percent a year or more, your investment is also likely to appreciate at that rate, or more.

4. It is perfectly liquid. If you need your money

back this afternoon for some reason, you can get it immediately.

5. All of your earnings are 100 percent tax-free. Every penny that you make you get to keep.

6. It does the dishes.

Only kidding about number 6, of course, but your chance of finding an investment with characteristics 1 through 5 is also, alas, just a dream. There is no way it could be otherwise. If an investment somehow appeared offering characteristics 2 through 5, say, it would immediately be recognized as so desirable that crowds would clamor to buy it, driving up its price so that characteristic 1 would not be true. But even that is a dream. No investment simultaneously offers characteristics 2 and 3. The potential for growth is always accompanied by the possibility of decline. In investing, you cannot have everything.

You can, however, have something, and it can be the thing that is just right for you. It is no difficult feat to find investments possessing any one (or even two or three) of our ideal characteristics. You can choose which characteristic is most important to you, and you can get it (even though you will have to accept the trade-off of not getting something else). If you want high current income from an investment, you can get it if you are willing to sacrifice the chance of its appreciating (increasing in value). If you're hoping for appreciation, you'll have to give up some safety. If you insist on safety, you'll have to give up some income. Every benefit has a price, but it will often be a price that you are willing to pay.

In many cases, deciding what you value most in an investment will be easy. If you are near retirement, you will want current income and safety, and you will not care very much about long-term growth potential. If you are young and gainfully employed, you will probably have the opposite concerns. If you are in a high tax bracket, then some kind of tax-advantaged investment will appeal to you. If you have a nervous stomach, you will value safety. If you enjoy gambling, then you enjoy gambling. Before you invest in anything, you should sit down with your broker and analyze your needs—both economic and emotional—to determine which investment vehicles are best suited to you.

The table on page 68 lists some investment opportunities and the characteristics they possess. You will note some of the trade-offs involved. No single investment has an X in every row.

Your choices are numerous, particularly in today's unregulated investment climate, but do not despair of being able to understand all your options. To begin, they all have one element in common. Every investment promises to deliver to you a future cash flow. You are laying out some money today (your "principal") that you have diverted, with some pain, from current consumption; in exchange you are receiving the right to participate in your chosen investment's future cash flow.

The arrangement can be very simple. You buy a federally guaranteed certificate of deposit (CD) from the bank on the corner, and you will receive a reliable cash flow of 8 percent, say, in the form of interest, for the life of the investment. (Then you get your principal back.) Or the arrangement may be more complex. You buy stock in a corporation and receive some cash flow in the form of dividends. You receive additional cash flow (you hope) in the form of capital appreciation as the price of the stock goes up. Your dividend cash flow is less than you would have received if you had taken the same amount of money and bought a certificate of deposit, but the capital appreciation cash flow (you hope) will more than make up the

x = Generally applicable
o = Depends on specific investment

Investment	INCOME NEEDS		GROWTH NEEDS		YOUR TEMPERAMENT		OTHER	
	High Yields	Security of Income	Potential for Short-Term Appreciation	Potential for Long-Term Appreciation	Security of Principal	Speculation	Liquidity	Tax Advantages
U.S. Treasury Securities		x			x		x	
Certificates of Deposit		x			x			
Money Market Mutual Funds		x			x		x	
Corporate Bonds	x	x			o		x	
Junk Bonds	x			x		x	x	
Preferred Stocks	x	x			o		x	
Convertible Securities	o	x	x	x	o		x	
Municipal Bonds		x			x		x	x
Discount Bonds	x	x		x	o		x	
Zero-Coupon Bonds	x				x		x	
Mortgage-Backed Securities	x	x			x		x	
Unit Investment Trusts	x	x			x		x	
Annuities	o	o		o	x		o	x
Precious Metals			x	x		x	x	
Collectibles				x		x		
Limited Partnerships	o	o		o			o	o
Mutual Funds	o	o	o	o	o	o	x	
Commodity Futures			x			x	x	
Common Stocks	o	o	x	x	o	o	x	
Real Estate	o	o	x		o	o		

difference. If the price of the stock goes down instead, you will be looking at a negative cash flow, which is not likely to make you very happy.

Naturally, you want as large a cash flow as possible in exchange for handing over your principal. This quest will lead you directly to the most basic of all investment trade-offs. The greater the potential cash flow from an investment, the greater the risk that it will not be delivered. You can put your money into a savings account and earn 5.25 percent a year guaranteed. You can put your money into a promising growth stock and make 50 percent a year as the stock moves up, or lose 50 percent a year as it moves down. You can put your money on Seabiscuit in the seventh and make 1,000 percent on your investment in a few minutes, unless you lose it all, which is far more likely.

Before people plop down their money for any investment, they tend to size up the risks involved. They will demand a higher rate of return from an investment that appears moderately safe than they will from an investment that appears very safe. That extra return is the reward they expect for accepting additional risk. Proprietors of uncertain ventures seeking investment dollars have no choice but to offer higher rates of return than, say, the United States Treasury.

This risk/reward trade-off figures in selecting between investment types and also in selecting particular investments within each investment category. Consider the choice between buying a corporate bond and investing in a piece of real estate. Corporate bonds may pay between 7 and 12 percent, as long as the issuing corporation stays solvent. A piece of real estate may appreciate 20 percent a year if yuppies move into the neighborhood, but it may decline in value if junkies head them off at the corner. If you buy the real estate, you're taking a chance—and looking at a greater potential cash flow in exchange for your willingness to take that chance.

But what if you decide to buy the corporate bond? Do you want the one paying 7 percent a year or the one paying 12 percent? Why do you think one is paying more than the other? Do you feel safer lending money to IBM, or to the Killer Bee Honey Corporation?

How much risk can you bear to live with? Surprisingly, the answer to that question does not always depend on how much risk a person can *afford* to live with. There are many very wealthy people who can well afford to take chances but who are emotionally incapable of living with the idea of losing money. There are, on the other hand, people of more moderate means who positively relish a flyer. You may have some idea where you fit on this spectrum, but people often discover their true feelings about risk only after they have stopped thinking about it in the abstract and actually put up some money. If after you have begun your investment program you find that you are kept awake nights worrying about what you might lose, then you have invested too speculatively. The best rule here is: Sell until you can sleep.

"LENDING" INVESTMENTS VS. "OWNING" INVESTMENTS

There are basically two things you can do with your investment money. You can lend it to somebody, or you can buy something with it.

When you put your money in a savings account, you are lending it to the bank. When you "buy" a certificate of deposit, you are still lending it to the bank. When you buy a corporate bond, you are lending your money to the corporation.

When you buy a share of common stock, however, you are buying a piece of the corporation and becoming a co-owner. When you buy real estate, or gold, or soybeans, or a mint-condition Captain Midnight decoder ring, you are becoming an owner not a lender.

As a general rule, lending your money is safer than buying something with it. Therefore, the rate of return you can expect to receive on "lending" investments will be lower than the potential rate of return on "owning" investments. It's the old risk/return trade-off.

Many "lending" investments are known as "fixed-income investments," because they pay a reliable and predictable rate of return. An 8 percent certificate of deposit will pay a steady 8 percent, risk-free. You can plan your family budget around that income, which is nice. But holders of fixed-income investments face another kind of risk. While an 8 percent certificate of deposit will never pay less than 8 percent, neither will it ever pay more—even if inflation should suddenly soar to 10 percent. In the late 1970s, many people found that they were actually losing money by holding what had once looked like "risk-free" fixed-income investments.

In the early 1980s, on the other hand, fixed-income investments fared very well relative to inflation. The inflation rate dropped, but investors were skeptical that it was down for good. Fearing that inflation would climb once again, they obtained interest rates on fixed-income investments that reflected past, not present, rates of inflation. By the time it was finally clear that inflation would stay down (at least for a while), many investors had locked in remarkably high "real" interest rates on long-term certificates of deposit and corporate and government bonds. (The "real" interest rate is the difference between an investment's interest rate and the rate of inflation.) In 1983, one bond index showed an average yield of 10.04 percent compared to a rise in consumer prices of 3.2 percent, for a "real" return of 6.84 percent. This compared with a negative real return of −3.92 percent in 1979, when the bonds were yielding 7.38 percent and inflation ran at 11.3 percent.

Historically, fixed-income investments have not performed all that well. They tend to run about 3 percentage points ahead of inflation (or ahead of what borrowers and lenders *expect* inflation to be). In periods of rapidly increasing inflation, they have often fallen behind. Nevertheless, they have faithfully continued to pay what they promised to pay, and the principal invested in them has generally been safe as well, even if its purchasing power was shrinking.

"Owning" investments, on the other hand, provide fewer guarantees. An "owning" investor's "downside" is not protected. The price of a stock, or an ounce of gold, or a decoder ring, can fall through the floor, endangering principal, to say nothing of interest. (No interest at all is paid on gold or decoder rings, and dividends on shares of stock rise and fall with corporate fortunes.) Yet neither is an "owning" investor's "upside" limited. A corporate bond pays what it pays and will never pay more, but a share of stock in that same corporation can soar to many times its original value if the corporation flourishes. "Lending" investments offer security against everything but the (real) risk of inflation. "Owning" investments offer the alluring promise of growth.

Experience has shown that "owning" investments—particularly stocks and real estate—are the best long-term investment vehicles for most people, and I will deal with each of them in subsequent chapters. Extremely speculative investments will get their own chapter after that. Meanwhile, the rest of this chapter will describe the most common "lending" investments, and a few assorted "owning" ones as well.

U.S. TREASURY SECURITIES

We're talking safety here. These are direct obligations of the United States government, which, if all else fails, can always tax somebody to raise the money to pay them off. Treasury securities come in several flavors:

Treasury bills: Issued in minimum denominations of $10,000, these mature in a year or less. They bear no stated interest rates. Instead, they are sold at auction for less than face (or "par") value. When they come due, their full par value is paid out.

Treasury notes: These are issued in minimums of $1,000 and mature in two to ten years. They bear stated interest rates, but they are also auctioned and may sell for less or more than face value, depending upon whether the stated interest rate is considered to be a good deal or not.

Treasury bonds: These are like notes in every way, except their maturity is ten years or more.

Because these securities are considered risk-free, they do not pay top-notch interest rates (it's the old risk/return trade-off). You can buy them directly from the government, which involves some paperwork, or from a broker, which involves some commission.

Probably the best-known government security is United States Savings Bonds, which many people remember from childhood school savings plans. Savings Bonds fell out of favor for a while, because the interest rates they offered were substantially below market rates. Today's Savings Bonds, however, are a better deal. Their interest rate is adjusted every six months (to 85 percent of the current rate on five-year Treasury notes). Savings Bonds are sold at a discount from their face value, like zero-coupon bonds (which are described below). Unlike other zero-coupon bonds, however, no federal income tax is due on interest earned until the bonds are cashed in. Moreover, the interest they pay, like that on other U.S. government securities, is exempt from state and local income taxes.

CERTIFICATES OF DEPOSIT (CDs)

We're still talking safety. CDs are issued by banks and savings and loan associations and pay reliable, fixed interest rates over set time periods. The principal invested is insured up to $100,000 by a government agency. The interest rates offered on CDs vary from week to week, depending on the issuer's guess about which way other interest rates are going. If *your* guess is that interest rates are on the way down, then buying a long-term CD is a safe way to lock in today's higher rate. If your guess is wrong, you will be stuck with a below-market rate until your CD's term is up.

The longer the term of the CD you buy, the higher the rate you will get. This is a consequence of the risk/return trade-off. Tying up your money for two years is riskier than tying it up for one year (there is more time for other interest rates to rise and make your CD look like a bad deal); you are rewarded for accepting the longer term with a slightly higher interest rate. If you want to cash in your CD early, either to put your money into a better investment or to cover emergency expenses, you will have to pay a penalty. Don't buy a CD, therefore, unless you are reasonably sure you will be willing and able to hold it to maturity. (Some brokers maintain "secondary markets" in CDs, which enable CD holders to sell their CDs to other investors instead of turning them in to the issuing institutions and paying the penalties. Sellers on the secondary market are, however, exposed to "market risk." For an explanation, see the section on discount bonds below.)

Note: CD rates are generally fixed for the term of the investment, but not always. In early 1985 a New York bank offered investors a choice. They could buy a regular one-year CD that paid 9.1 percent. Or they could buy a floating-rate CD that paid 8.9 percent. If interest rates went up, the floating CD rate would go up too, as high as 9.65 percent. (It would never go below 8.9 percent, however.) The element of gambling that lurks beneath the surface of all investments was thus brought out into the open. Did you expect interest rates to go up? (They did not, by the way.) Were you willing to wager .2 percent of your CD on it?

MONEY MARKET MUTUAL FUNDS

Mutual funds are investment pools that sell shares to small investors, enabling them to participate in investments they could not afford to buy on their own. Money market mutual funds are a specialized type of mutual fund. They invest only in "money market instruments" —short-term loans to banks, governments, and major corporations. Until money market funds came along, there was no way most individual investors could participate in the

money market, where the smallest loans going are for
$100,000. Now investors of moderate means can lend out
their money on the same terms as the rich (minus, of
course, a small cut off the top for the managers of the
money market funds).

The interest paid on money market funds is often slightly
lower than the interest paid on CDs, but money funds
offer several advantages over CDs:

- They are perfectly liquid. You can get your money out
  at any time with no penalty.
- Interest (called dividends, because you are technically
  buying stock in an investment company when you put
  your money into a money market fund) is paid daily. If
  you like, it can be automatically reinvested at current
  rates. All of this is recorded in monthly statements.
- Many money market funds allow you to withdraw funds
  by writing checks (generally in amounts of $500 or more).
  If you make your mortgage payments, say, with a money
  market check, you are keeping your money at work,
  earning money market rates, until the day the check
  clears.

These are the drawbacks of money market funds:

- Your investment is not insured. (But the securities that
  money market funds invest in are so safe that money
  funds are still considered almost risk-free.)
- Interest rates vary daily, depending on money market
  conditions. If you think rates are on the way down, you
  would be better off in a CD, where you can lock in
  today's interest rate for a year or longer.
- Compared to many other investments, money market
  rates are low. You should therefore use a money market

fund only as a place to keep reserve cash, as a sort of high-ticket checking account, as a place to hold your investment dollars between more permanent investments, or as a place to hold investment dollars while interest rates are rising (and you are waiting for longer-term investments to begin reflecting those higher rates). You should not think of a money market fund as a long-term investment itself. You can do better elsewhere.

CORPORATE BONDS

To finance their operations, corporations are always borrowing money. Much of that money is borrowed from the general public through the issuance of corporate bonds. These bonds generally pay a fixed interest rate over a fixed term. Interest payments are usually made to the bondholders every six months. At the end of the term, the bondholders' principal is refunded.

The interest rates paid on corporate bonds vary according to the term of the bonds (the longer the term, the higher the rate) and according to the creditworthiness of the issuing corporation. If you are considering buying bonds, you don't have to investigate a corporation's finances yourself; several financial service organizations (including Standard & Poor's and Moody's) issue widely used letter grades rating bond issues. Another factor affecting the interest rate on a particular issue is whether the bond is backed by specific assets of the corporation (which decreases the bond buyer's risk) or is a "debenture," backed only by the company's general credit and good name.

Corporate bonds usually pay higher rates than money market funds or certificates of deposit, and they are an excellent way of locking in high interest rates when credit is tight. (Some high-quality bonds paid as much as 18 percent in 1981.) There is, however, a catch to this business of locking in high rates. The fine print on many bonds specifies that they can be "called," or redeemed, before maturity. If a corporation issues a twenty-year bond paying, say, 12 percent and two years later the interest rate on comparable new issues has fallen to 8 percent, that corporation will be a little glum about the prospect of paying above-market-rate interest for the next eighteen years. If the bond issue is callable, the corporation will simply redeem the bonds at face value (or, sometimes, at a premium), say thank you to the nice bondholders for lending their money for two years at 12 percent, and promptly launch a new 8 percent bond issue to replace the money it has just paid out. (The company would be happy, of course, to sell those 8 percent bonds to the former holders of the 12 percent bonds; those individuals, however, may be less than happy about the whole situation.) As interest rates fell after the peaks of the early 1980s, many corporate bonds were called—including many issues that had appeared to be "call protected" by anticall language in the fine print. "Investors who believe they have noncall or nonrefund protection shouldn't be lulled into complacency," a financial analyst told *The New York Times*. "Any clever financial executive can find his way around such . . . restrictions."

A special category of corporate bonds are "convertible" issues, which can be exchanged for a specified number of shares of the issuing corporation's common stock. Convertible bondholders thus share in the growth potential offered by stock (if the price of a company's stock goes up, the value of bonds that may be exchanged for that stock naturally increases too), while still enjoying the relative security and stable interest rates of a bond. Because they have these advantages, convertible bonds generally pay lower interest rates than ordinary bonds.

One option for a small investor interested in corporate bonds is to buy shares in a bond mutual fund. Like any mutual fund, bond funds pool the resources of many investors to buy a diverse group of securities. That diversification lends safety to mutual fund investments. For $1,000, a small investor can buy a single corporate bond, or she can put the money into a bond mutual fund and indirectly buy a small share in each of thousands of different corporate bonds. Her eggs are in many baskets. Some bond mutual funds invest only in issues from the highest-rated corporations. Others seek out higher-yielding bonds from shakier companies. It's the old risk/return trade-off. You pays your money and you takes your choice.

"JUNK BONDS"

So-called junk bonds are a relatively high-risk version of corporate bonds. They are bonds issued by companies with very high, and potentially unhealthy, levels of debt. Among such companies in recent years have been those involved in "leveraged buy-outs." In a leveraged buy-out (known, in the trade, as an LBO), a group of investors or corporate managers buys all the outstanding shares of stock in a corporation and "takes it private." Buying all that stock costs the new owners an enormous amount of money, which they often do not have on hand. They may borrow it from the public by issuing junk bonds in the name of their newly acquired company.

Many of these bonds entail a significant risk that the

issuing companies will not be able to keep up the interest payments. To compensate bond buyers for this risk, these issues pay interest rates considerably higher than those on more secure corporate bonds. This is the great attraction of junk bonds, and it has induced many investors to buy them. Their sale has been promoted by advertisements for junk bond mutual funds that focus on the high interest rates being paid. Such mutual funds may, in fact, be the best way to buy junk bonds, since investing in many different issues somewhat diminishes the risk associated with these securities.

PREFERRED STOCKS

These are securities that look like stocks but function like bonds. Like bonds, preferred stocks are issued with a designated "par value" and a specified rate of return. That return is paid by the issuing corporations in the form of dividends, an area in which preferred stockholders get "preferred" treatment. Corporations are obligated to pay preferred stock dividends before any dividends are paid to holders of common stock (but *after* interest payments have been made on corporate bonds). Similarly, if a company goes broke, preferred stockholders have second claim on its assets, after creditors (who include bondholders) but before owners of common stock. Many preferred stock issues are "cumulative," which means that if dividends are skipped any year (or years), all dividends, past and present, must be paid in full before any common stock dividends can be paid. Some preferred stock is also "convertible" into shares of common stock any time the shareholder pleases.

Corporations enjoy certain tax benefits from owning the preferred stock of other corporations. Corporations therefore bid up the price of preferred stock to reflect those benefits. This makes preferred stock, in most cases, a noncompetitive investment for individuals.

MUNICIPAL BONDS

These are similar to corporate bonds, only they are issued instead by the governments of cities, states, and United States territories, and by agencies of those governments. As with corporate bonds, the creditworthiness of the issuers is graded by bond rating services, and interest rates vary according to those ratings and the length of term. Many municipals are callable, and they may be purchased via municipal bond mutual funds.

The great appeal of municipal bonds is that the interest they earn is free of federal income tax. (They are also generally free of local income taxes within the states in which they are issued.) This makes municipal bonds extremely attractive to investors in the higher tax brackets. To an investor in the 33 percent bracket, a municipal bond paying 8 percent is worth exactly as much as a corporate bond paying 12 percent. Municipal bond issuers are therefore able to market their bonds at lower rates than corporations. You'll have to sit down and work out your own tax situation to decide if municipal bonds are a good buy for you.

Note: Municipal bonds are a *bad* buy for IRAs and Keogh plans. Why accept a lower interest rate in exchange for a tax-free return when *any* bonds you buy for your IRA are automatically tax-free until you withdraw the funds? At that point, the money you withdraw from your IRA *will* be taxed, even if it derived from municipal bonds.

DISCOUNT BONDS

Bonds, both corporate and municipal, need not be held to maturity by those who own them. They are freely transferable and may be sold at any time for whatever any buyer is willing to pay.

What will a buyer pay? That depends on the interest rate of the bond in question and how it compares with current interest rates. Suppose you own a high-quality $1,000 corporate bond paying 10 percent interest ($100 a year) and you decide to sell it at a time when comparable new bond issues are paying 12 percent. Clearly, no one of normal intelligence will pay you $1,000 for your bond when that same $1,000 could buy a new bond paying the higher rate. Someone might, however, be willing to pay $833 for your bond (the $100 annual interest he or she will receive is 12 percent of $833). Your bond would thus sell at a discount to reflect the change in interest rates. The $1,000 principal on your bond is still secure, but only if you hold it to maturity. By selling it sooner you have subjected yourself to "market risk," and you have lost.

You can also win at this game, if interest rates have gone down. A $1,000 10 percent bond will be worth $1,250 if interest rates decline to 8 percent.

Why might you want to buy a discount bond? It is, first of all, a reliable investment paying current interest rates (because you can always buy it at a discount, or premium, reflecting those rates). Second, there's always a chance that interest rates will go down, which means that the value of your bond will go up and you can sell it at a profit. Third, when the bond reaches its maturity, the issuing corporation or government will pay you its full face value, no matter what you paid for it. (This guaranteed profit is, however, figured into the market prices of discount bonds.) Finally, if you want to own bonds but avoid market risk, you can find and buy discount bonds that are due to mature exactly when you're going to need your money back (for example, the year your daughter goes to college). This eliminates the possibility that you will have to sell the bonds for less than you paid for them.

ZERO-COUPON BONDS

A lot of attention has been devoted to this "new" investment vehicle in recent years, although there is nothing truly new about it. U.S. Savings Bonds have always been a form of zero-coupon bond. That is, they do not make periodic interest payments to those who own them. Instead, you buy them at a discount off their face value. When they mature, you are given the full face value. In effect, you get all your interest at the end, in one lump sum.

This is the principle of zero-coupon bonds. (Their name derives from the fact that most traditional bonds used to come with a set of coupons attached. You clipped one off every six months and turned it in to receive your interest payment.) While a traditional twenty-year, 10 percent, $1,000 bond will cost you $1,000 and send you a check for $50 every six months, a twenty-year, 10 percent, $1,000 "zero" will cost you $149 and pay you nothing for twenty years. Then it will pay you $1,000.

Turning $149 into $1,000 sounds like a pretty good deal, doesn't it? It's just one more demonstration of the remarkable powers of compound interest. And it's directly related to the one great advantage of zero-coupon bonds. Unlike ordinary bonds, zeroes guarantee not only to pay you the specified interest rate on your principal; they also guarantee to pay it on your interest. To understand why this is important, consider what would happen if you bought that traditional 10 percent $1,000 bond and interest rates then fell to 7 percent. You'd get your 10 percent interest on the bond, all right, in the form of $50 every six months. But what kind of return would you get if you proceeded to reinvest that $50? Just 7 percent. If you had bought the zero-coupon bond instead, your $50 in interest would be automatically reinvested at 10 percent, no matter what the current interest rate was. Zero-coupon bonds are thus the best possible way to lock in high interest rates far into the future. (The flip side of this is that if interest rates go up after you buy your bond, nobody is going to want to touch it with a ten-foot pole.)

Zero-coupon bonds are issued by corporations, by states and local governments, and by the United States Treasury. In addition, several brokerage houses have created their own zero-coupon issues based on traditional federal government securities.

If you decide to invest in zeros, you should keep in mind that some issues can be called early, not at their face value but according to a graduated redemption schedule. And note also that although no annual interest payments are made to you, the Internal Revenue Service will tax you as if they were (except for tax-free municipal zero-coupon bonds). You might therefore want to consider taxable zero-coupon bonds only for your IRA and Keogh plans.

MORTGAGE-BACKED SECURITIES

Mortgages are generally nice safe investments for lenders, but it used to be that only banks, savings and loan associations, and other institutions could own them. These entities lent money to homeowners and then sat around for thirty years while the borrowers (in most cases) reliably repaid them.

Today, anyone can be a mortgage lender by investing in mortgage-backed securities. The best known of these are "Ginnie Maes," issued by the Government National Mortgage Association (GNMA). The GNMA assembles pools of federally insured mortgages and then sells shares in those pools. Investors receive a proportionate share of the payments made on those mortgages. The smallest unit sold by GNMA costs $25,000, but investors may buy into GNMAs indirectly by putting as little as $1,000 or so into a GNMA mutual fund or unit trust.

Ginnie Maes are very safe, because they are guaranteed by the U.S. government, and they also pay relatively high interest rates. This seeming exception to the risk/return trade-off is a result of two things:

First of all, Ginnie Maes are "self-liquidating." Every month, Ginnie Mae owners receive payments that include both interest and a piece of their principal back. If interest rates are falling, it will be difficult to reinvest that returned principal at as high a rate as the Ginnie Mae. Second, if home mortgage rates are declining, some of the people whose home mortgages make up the Ginnie Mae pool may decide to pay off their mortgages and refinance. So Ginnie Mae holders may find their investment paying off ahead of schedule into an environment of lower interest rates.

Mortgage-backed securities similar to Ginnie Maes are also sold by "Freddie Mac" (the Federal Home Loan Mortgage Corporation) and "Fannie Mae" (the Federal National Mortgage Association). Some privately packaged mortgage-backed securities are also available.

A recent new wrinkle in mortgage-backed securities is the "collateralized mortgage obligation (CMO)." CMOs are bonds backed by mortgages. As bonds, they are more predictable than GNMAs. They are issued with defined maturity dates, at which time one's original investment is repaid in full. One can count on receiving interest payments until that date and then recovering one's principal without encountering "market risk." (Like discount bonds, the price of a GNMA will dip if interest rates go up.)

UNIT INVESTMENT TRUSTS

Unit investment trusts are similar to mutual funds in that they are pools of investments assembled by professional money managers and sold in shares to individual investors. They are unlike mutual funds in that they are one-shot deals. While a mutual fund will live forever (or try to), constantly adjusting and expanding and renewing its portfolio, a unit investment trust will assemble a fixed portfolio, sell shares in it, and then lock up.

Unit trusts assemble and sell shares in corporate bonds, municipal bonds, government securities, Ginnie Maes, or other investment vehicles. Each unit trust is assembled with a specific investment goal in mind (one may consist entirely of municipal bonds issued within a particular state, for example, so that the interest earned will be free of all taxes for residents of that state). Like mutual funds, unit trusts provide security through diversification. Like some mutual funds, unit trusts generally charge buyers a sales commission of several percent. You should therefore plan on holding your shares in a unit trust for the long haul. The commission will eat away your profits if you trade in and out.

ANNUITIES

Annuities, which are created by insurance companies and marketed by insurance companies and brokers, have deservedly become very popular of late, because they offer the same great tax advantage of an IRA—tax-deferred compounding—and, unlike an IRA, there is no annual limit on the amount you can put into an annuity.

You can buy an annuity with a single lump-sum payment or with a series of payments spread out over time. And you have your choice of two kinds of annuities—fixed or variable.

In a fixed annuity, the money you give the insurance company is invested as it sees fit. It doesn't really matter to you what they do with it, because the company guarantees to pay into your account a specified "fixed" rate of return. With a variable annuity, on the other hand, you tell the company how you want your money invested. Generally, you are offered a choice of stock, bond, and money market mutual funds. You are often allowed to switch freely (and without paying taxes) from one fund to another. The rate of return your annuity earns will vary with the success (and the relative risk) of the investments you choose.

With either a fixed or a variable annuity, the money in

your account compounds tax-free as long as you leave it there. As we have seen, that means it will grow at a far healthier rate than an ordinary, taxed investment. If you put $20,000 into an annuity earning 8 percent annually, at the end of twenty years you will have $93,219. If you had put the same $20,000 into a non-tax-deferred investment also paying 8 percent, you would have only $56,825 at the end of the same period (assuming you are in the 33 percent tax bracket.) Taxes will be payable on your annuity income when you withdraw it, but the benefit of years of tax-free compounding will leave you still ahead. If you withdraw your entire annuity in one lump sum, your tax bill will be $24,162 (that's 33 percent of $73,219; you paid tax on your $20,000 in principal before you put it in). That will leave you with $69,057—$12,232 more than the non-tax-deferred investment.

In fact, you will probably do better than that, because by the time you retire you are likely to be in a lower tax bracket. And you are unlikely, in any case, to withdraw your annuity all at once. The majority of annuities are paid out in fixed monthly payments beginning sometime after retirement age. You choose when they begin. You also choose how long you want the payments to run: until you die; until you and your spouse both die; for a specified number of years or until you die, whichever is longer; or simply for a specified number of years. (If your annuity payments outlive you, they will go to your heirs.) The size of the monthly payout naturally varies with the option you choose; longer payout periods pay less each month than shorter ones. Most people, sensibly, choose one of the options that guarantees them a monthly income for the rest of their lives.

Annuities are best set up by someone thinking ahead to retirement, since there are tax penalties for withdrawal of your earnings before age 59½, and there may be penalty charges as well by annuity sponsors for withdrawals before a specified number of years have elapsed. Annuity sponsors may also charge annual maintenance fees, which reduce the annuity's effective yield. So read the fine print.

LIMITED PARTNERSHIPS

Limited partnerships are a form of business organization in which an enterprise is owned by one general partner and many limited partners. The general partner organizes and manages the venture and sells shares to the limited partners, who put up the money.

In exchange for their investment, the limited partners generally receive a steady income from a type of business they could not have entered on their own. Limited partnerships commonly involve real estate, oil and gas drilling, motion picture production, or industrial equipment leasing. Before the 1986 tax reform, many limited partnerships existed primarily to offer tax shelters for wealthy investors. Today the tax advantages of limited partnerships are vastly reduced (but not totally eliminated), and limited partnerships should be evaluated on the conventional standards of risk and return.

A typical equipment leasing limited partnership will pool the investments of its many limited partners and purchase millions of dollars worth of industrial equipment, which it will then lease to corporations. All the limited partners will receive a proportionate share of the lease payments. When the leases expire and the partnership is dissolved (typically after five to ten years), the equipment will be sold and the limited partners will receive shares of the money it brings. All money earned by the partnership "passes through" to the partners; the partnership entity itself pays no income taxes. A share of all partnership income is, however, taken by the general partner as a management fee. Potential limited partners should determine the size of that fee and decide whether it is fair. The success or failure of a limited partnership depends on the business acumen of the general partner, so potential limited partners should also determine if there is reason to believe that the general partner knows what he is doing.

One drawback of limited partnerships is that they tend to be "illiquid." That is, it may be difficult to get your money out of a limited partnership by selling your share before the partnership dissolves itself. The typical minimum initial investment in a limited partnership is $2,000 to $5,000. If you may need that money before the end of the projected lifetime of the partnership, you should not put it in.

A new wrinkle in limited partnerships in recent years has been created in the form of the "master limited partnership." Right off the bat, master limited partnerships (MLPs) have a couple of advantages over traditional limited partnerships for small investors. MLPs are sold in relatively low-priced units, like shares of a mutual fund, and they are traded on major stock exchanges, so they can be bought or sold at any time.

Like traditional limited partnerships, MLPs are managed by a general partner who has sold shares to the public. MLPs may consist of a bunch of old limited partnerships, which have been consolidated into one "master" limited partnership. They may consist of one part of a corporation, which the corporation has decided to "roll out" as a limited partnership. (An example of this is a paper company that sold partnership interests in its timberland harvest program.) Or an MLP may consist of an entire business that has converted itself from corporate form into a limited partnership. The best-known example of this is the Boston Celtics.

Individuals who buy MLP shares are generally looking for a high rate of return on their money. MLPs are able to pay high rates because MLPs pay no income tax themselves but pass through all earnings to the partners, because not all the money passed through to partners is immediately taxable, and because MLPs tend to distribute everything they earn. In addition, MLP organizers sometimes promise to pay a guaranteed rate of return for a specified number of years.

One drawback of MLPs is that, in order to keep limited partners happy by passing out a lot of cash, the general partner may not retain enough cash *in* the business to keep it healthy. Potential investors in MLPs should consider that prospect. They should also evaluate the general business outlook for the MLP enterprise and the track record of the MLP sponsor. Does the sponsoring organization have an ongoing commitment to make the MLP venture succeed, or is it just unloading a business in which it will have no substantial further interest?

GOLD AND SILVER

Precious metals are popular investments, especially during periods of high inflation, because they, like other commodities, tend to increase in value at the inflation rate. They are, after all, *things*, and an increase in the price of things is the definition of inflation.

Gold has special characteristics, however, that set it

apart from other commodities. It has a long heritage of use as money, possessing ideal traits for the role: It is scarce, transportable, nonperishable, and divisible. It is also highly liquid, easily sold at current market prices anywhere in the world, so it has traditionally been used to store wealth by people living in societies suffering economic or political instability. This link between the popularity of gold and political or economic crisis is reflected even in stable countries like the United States. One brochure published by a major American brokerage house advises investors, "In times of heightened concern over political conflict or general business health, gold and silver investments can be extremely profitable." (Presumably, a nuclear war would be *great* for the gold market.)

Investors in gold are thus in a sense betting against the well-being of their fellow citizens. Despite that, or because of it, many investors like to keep at least a small share of their assets in gold or in silver (which is like gold, only less so). Precious metals do provide excellent protection against inflation, and, if a tidal wave ever washes over the United States, survivors swimming to South America carrying gold coins in their teeth will be politely received.

There are several ways to invest in gold:

- Gold bullion.
- Gold coins issued by the United States, Mexico, Canada, China, and other countries.
- Stock in gold mining companies.
- Precious metals portfolios (similar to mutual funds) organized by brokerage houses.
- Gold futures (for a description of futures, see Chapter 9).

The main drawback of owning actual gold (bullion or coins) is that the stuff just sits there. It doesn't create wealth or give you a share in the creation of wealth, and it doesn't earn interest. In fact, it costs you money for storage and insurance.

COLLECTIBLES

Collectibles, which include antiques, paintings, rare coins and stamps, and even back-issue comic books, are another popular investment during inflationary times, and the prices of some of them have soared out of sight. (A Van Gogh painting of a vase of sunflowers recently sold at auction for $39.9 million. And have you priced a Louis XIV credenza lately?) But collectibles are an especially tricky investment because of the little item known as "spread," which is the gap between the net buying price and the net selling price of a thing. If gold is currently going for $400 an ounce, you can buy an ounce for $400 (plus a few dollars for a dealer's commission) or you can sell an ounce for $400 (minus a few dollars for a dealer's commission). Either way, your net price will be pretty close to $400. The spread is small.

Collectibles don't work that way. Most collectibles are sold in retail stores, whose proprietors expect, and get, a conventional retail markup on their merchandise. An antique spinning wheel that a dealer is selling for $400 may have *cost* the dealer only $200. If you buy that spinning wheel for $400, and the value of antiques proceeds to increase a full 100 percent, that same dealer will be happy to buy the spinning wheel back from you—for $400. Prices have to double for you to break even.

The spreads in all collectibles are not this wide, and they can be somewhat reduced by buying and selling at auctions and in private sales, but collectibles are still a tough area in which to realize a profit.

This is partly because the market for many collectibles is a "thin" one, with far fewer people standing always ready to buy and sell than there are in "thick" markets, like those for stocks and bonds. You can always find a thousand people interested in buying your shares of Xerox. You can't be sure of finding a crowd interested in your collection of Rudolph Valentino autographs.

With that in mind, go right out and buy modern American art, or Icelandic commemoratives, or rare first editions of Beetle Bailey. But buy only things that you enjoy owning, because the psychic rewards you get from having your collectibles in your living room may be the only rewards you ever see from them. If they do appreciate, consider it a bonus—not an entitlement.

THE NEED TO DIVERSIFY

That should be enough investment alternatives to hold you for a while. Can't decide which one to buy? Good. Because you shouldn't buy just one. Diversification is the best way you have to reduce risk in an unpredictable world. Most investors will want portfolios that combine some current income with some chance for long-term growth, some liquidity and some of the high yields available in nonliquid investments, some rock-solid securities and a couple of high flyers. Look at Table 5-1 again. You don't want all your X's in a single row.

Now, on to the stock market. . . .

CHAPTER 6

THE STOCK MARKET

THE LONG-TERM VIEW

It's a nice fantasy to imagine what your bank account would look like today if you had been around and buying stocks following the Great Crash of 1929. In the aftermath of that spectacular stock market collapse, which saw paper fortunes crumble into dust and investors head for the windows of tall buildings, the prices of common stocks sank to amazing lows. An investor with surviving resources, great foresight, and a strong stomach could have picked up shares of General Motors for $9 apiece (1987 value: $60) or IBM for $68 (1987 value, adjusted for splits: $46,000).

But what if you had bought stock shortly *before* the Great Crash? What if you had bought into the market at precisely the wrong time, when stock prices had been driven to then-record highs in a roaring bull market by the doomed owners of pyramiding paper fortunes? How would you stand today if you had bought stock at those inflated pre-Crash prices and held it ever since?

Just fine.

Over the past sixty years, the average share of common stock listed on the New York Stock Exchange has appreciated (assuming you reinvested dividends) at a compound annual rate of about 10 percent. This average takes into account the stocks of companies that have gone out of business, and, remarkably, it is only a little bit lower (about 9 percent) if it is figured for a portfolio purchased shortly before the Great Crash. (It is, of course, significantly higher—about 14 percent—if figured for a portfolio purchased shortly *after* the Great Crash.) These figures which held true even after the stock market crash of October 1987, compare with a compound annual inflation rate over the same years of about 3 percent, and a compound rate of return on corporate bonds of just over 4 percent. Historically, stocks have been an outstanding investment.

This has been for two reasons:

1. Stock prices tend, at the very least, to keep pace with inflation, because shares of stock represent shares of real things owned and produced by the issuing corporations, and an increase in the price of such things *is* inflation.

2. American corporations have done an excellent job of mobilizing people, technology, and natural resources to create wealth, and stock issued by those corporations appreciates to reflect that wealth creation. One common measure of corporate wealth creation is the statistic known as "return on equity." "Equity," in this case, refers to a corporation's net worth; "return" is profit. The average annual return on equity of American corporations over the last sixty years has been about 10 percent. It is no coincidence that the stock of those corporations has appreciated at the same rate.

The long-term advantages of stocks may seem dubious when the stock market hits the skids, but it is at those times that it is most important to think in the long term. In October 1987, stock prices collapsed in a frightening rush and landed at about the level they had occupied a year earlier. A year earlier, investors had been thrilled to have their stocks reach that level. During the intervening months, as stocks roared up in one of the greatest bull markets in history, some investors made the mistake of thinking the good times would last indefinitely. But the market *always* turns. When it did, in remarkably dramatic fashion, it took cool perspective to remember that the very prices then being bemoaned had been celebrated a year before. People who had been investing steadily over a period of years (the bull market had begun in 1982) may have had their illusions shattered, but not their net worth. Most still held substantial profits.

The big losers were people who had been attempting to "play" the market during its great upward leap, jumping in and out for short-term gains. When the market crashed, they learned very painfully that playing the market is a dangerous mistake.

DO NOT "PLAY" THE MARKET

There are two reasons people lose money in the stock market. One has to do with the stocks they choose to buy, or when they choose to buy them. Simply put, they buy the wrong stock, or they buy the right stock at the wrong time.

We'll talk about that in a moment, but first we must deal with the other reason people lose money in the stock market. That is: They forget why they're there.

You should enter the stock market for one reason only: to associate your capital with wealth-creating enterprises. This may sound too obvious to mention—why else does someone buy a share of stock?—but in fact this goal is often forgotten by people who should know better. This is partly a result of the necessary abstractions of modern life. When you buy a share of Chrysler, nobody comes to your house and hands you the unpainted door of a Dodge. That may be approximately what you have just purchased, but it would hardly be an efficient way to do business to let every stockholder in a corporation take his or her piece of the company home every night. Instead, the assets of a corporation are recorded in the shorthand of numbers, and ownership shares of the corporation are represented by pieces of paper with numbers on them. These "securities" are what change hands on the nation's stock exchanges, and people tend to talk about them as if they themselves were the things being invested in. In fact, when you buy stock in a corporation you are buying a share of vast material assets and a complex human organization. What you *see* is a piece of paper.

These pieces of paper change hands on Wall Street and elsewhere. Sometimes they are sold at a profit and sometimes they are sold at a loss. Often a security passes through dozens of hands without anyone involved ever laying eyes on the very real assets the paper represents. People who own the paper keep track of its price by looking at numbers on other pieces of paper, and there is often no clear and immediate connection between changes in that price and changes in the real world represented by the stock certificate. The price goes up, the price goes down. It begins to feel like an enormous game of chance— Las Vegas with ticker machines. Everybody knows somebody who has made a fortune in electronics stocks—and he can't tell a transistor from a toaster. So what does it matter what is happening back at the factories and stores represented by the stock certificates? On Wall Street you can trade pieces of paper, and make a lot of money doing it.

Now, it is true that fortunes have been made trading those pieces of paper with hardly a thought given to what they represent. And it's very easy to get caught up in it all—hanging around brokerage offices watching the ticker, asking, "What's the word on the street?," wondering "Which way is the market going?" You may get lucky for a while. If you have entered the market during one of its periodic great advances, you will do very well indeed, buying one stock, holding it for a while, selling it at a profit, buying another, repeating the process. When the market begins one of its periodic declines, you will not do so well, unless you are one of the rare geniuses who can tell precisely when the switch in direction has arrived. (It's a Wall Street saying that "they don't ring a bell at the top of the market.")

In the long run, you are going to lose. If you get caught up in the game of trading pieces of paper for a profit, you will find yourself making a lot of trades. You will try to buy stocks that are about to go up in price, and you will try to sell stocks that are about to go down. Every time you make a trade, you will be buying from somebody, or selling to somebody. It is very easy to forget this—that there is another human being on the other side of every trade you make—because, the way the market works, you almost never know who that other person is. But you should always remember that you are dealing with another person, and that it is a person who thinks you are wrong. He has decided to sell the stock you have decided to

buy. You think it's underpriced and about to move up.
He thinks it's a turkey and it's time to bail out. One of
you will turn out to be right and one will turn out to
be wrong. One of you will lose; the other will win. You
can't both win; short-term stock trading is a zero-sum
game, where one side's gains are equal to the other's
losses.

How often do you think you can win? By the law of
averages, you should win half the time. But, if you do win
half the time, you will still lose, because you are paying
brokerage commissions every time you trade. (The law of
averages doesn't have to pay brokerage commissions.) To
come out ahead, you have to win more than half the time.
More often than not, you have to be right while the
people on the other side of your trades are wrong. But
who are these people whom you must consistently out-
smart? Are they a bunch of blithering idiots? ("Only a
moron would sell that stock with the market moving the
way it is!") In fact, they're probably reasonably intelligent
people. They're probably just as smart as you. And some
of them are undoubtedly smarter. Some of them are self-
made millionaires who have made their fortunes in the
stock market over many years of trading. Some of them
are the managers of vast mutual funds, who have batteries
of computers and battalions of well-trained analysts guiding their every move. Some of them may even be executives of the very corporations whose stock you are buying
and selling.

Who are you?

Well, you may say, I've got some expert advice in
my corner too. I have this broker who really seems to
know what she's doing. Last month alone she made me
$1,200.

That's nice, but if she's so smart how come she's not

rich? Why isn't she cabling in her own market orders from her yacht off Bimini? How come she has to work for you?

Neither she nor anyone else knows which way the market is going over the short term. Anyone who says they have figured it out is deluded, or mistaken, or dishonest.

Trying to win the short-term game in the stock market can be tremendously exciting. But you had better decide right now whether you want to get rich or you want to have fun. If you enjoy matching your wits against others and absorbing yourself in complex intellectual games, I recommend you take up bridge or chess. They're not quite as much fun as the stock market, but they're a whole lot cheaper.

The path you should take in the stock market—*investing*—is a slow and often boring one. It requires patience and discipline and a lot of waiting. It's not nearly as much fun as attempting to trade pieces of paper at a profit, but it does offer one nice consolation: It can help you achieve your goal of financial serenity.

PICKING STOCKS

Investing in stocks is a positive-sum game (one in which all the players can come out ahead), because over the long term most American corporations create real wealth and the prices of their stock rise to reflect that wealth creation. Nevertheless, there are some real stinkers out there. There are stocks that go down and then down some more; there are companies that go belly-up. The 10 percent average annual appreciation of American stocks over the last six decades has been calculated by combining the records of companies that have prospered immensely, single-handedly making their shareholders wealthy, with those of companies that have tortured their shareholders with endlessly declining fortunes.

Which stocks are you going to buy?

The first step (but only the first step) in making that decision is identifying a good company. The bad ones don't wear little signs saying "I am a stinker," but the good ones do possess certain identifiable characteristics. Dean Witter summed them up in a 1963 speech: "I shall again repeat the hackneyed advice to recommend stocks of good, well-known, and well-established companies with a long history of successful operation."

Picking such companies is really just a matter of common sense. You want a company with honest, effective managers that is producing a product or service that people want and need. The company should be offering that product or service to the market at an attractive price, and it should have demonstrated its mastery of the many steps in the chain between the creation of a product and its delivery to the consumer. The company should be comfortable with complexity and uncertainty, and it should be able to adapt to change, because there will be significant changes in its field, whatever its field may be. The company should have an enlightened attitude toward its own employees, and it should have its financial house in order.

You may know of such companies through your own direct experience. Perhaps you work for one, or buy things from one. You may read about such companies in your local newspaper or in the financial press. Your broker will certainly have some candidates to recommend, backed by detailed analyses prepared by the research department of the brokerage firm.

You may want to investigate your candidate companies further by inspecting their annual reports. Of course, according to most annual reports, every company is a great company—or so say the opening letters from management that are pasted between the glossy photographs of smiling employees. There are a few honest exceptions. A couple of years ago an Oregon high-technology company called Tektronix amazed annual-report aficionados by acknowledging, "That dill-pickle look on your face says you have just read our Highlights, as they are euphemistically called. . . . Our earnings took a pasting." But such candor is rare. More typical is this line from an Eastern Airlines annual report: "The quarter's earnings contained a substantial contribution from a settlement arising from the involuntary termination of operating equipment." Translated, this meant: "If the plane hadn't crashed we would have been in the red. Fortunately no one was killed. The insurance company paid more for the plane than we had depreciated it to."

To get the most out of annual reports, you should read them like Chinese newspapers, from back to front. It's in the back, amid the financial tables and their attendant fine-print footnotes, that you may find warning signs about the company's health. Among the things to look for here is the ratio of the company's assets to its debt; a healthy ratio is generally at least two to one. This figure may be distorted, however, by the inclusion of some dubious assets. If a significant share of assets are listed under the heading "intangibles," check the footnotes to see what those intangibles are. A company may put a higher price tag on its "goodwill" than anyone else would.

Another component of a company's assets is its inventory of unsold goods. If the inventory is only a small fraction of the company's annual sales, that indicates that inventories are moving out at a respectable pace and are almost certainly worth what the company says they are. If the inventory is building up, on the other hand, because nobody wants to buy slide rules anymore, then the inventory's value may be overstated.

One of the most widely cited figures in a company's financial statement is its earnings per share (of stock outstanding). It's very nice if earnings per share go up at a steady rate (consult previous years' annual reports to check on this and other trends). But take note of whether increased earnings come from normal product sales, or if they come from some extraordinary sale that may have been made just to pump up earnings. A company should be selling a larger number of its products every year. It can only sell its headquarters building once.

WHAT IS A STOCK WORTH?

Assuming you have done your homework and have identified some successful, healthy, honest corporations, should you rush right out and buy their stocks? Not necessarily. You may be the ten millionth person this week to identify that company as a winner. Nine million of those people may already be in the market trying to buy the stock, waving hundred-dollar bills around and bidding up its price.

The stock of a good company is not a good buy at any price. It is only a good buy if it is available at a price equal to or less than its proportionate share of the company's value. Granted, value is a somewhat subjective term, but at least it is grounded in reality. What dividend is the company paying? What is its net worth (its assets minus its debts)? What are its prospects for the future? All of these are components of value.

Price, unlike value, is a completely subjective concept. It is whatever somebody is willing to pay for something at a given moment. It is subject to individual whims and to the many kinds of mass psychology that move the stock market through its cycles. Wall Street continuously abounds with significant disparities between price and value. These disparities will give you the chance to make some excellent investments, *if* you are capable of independent thinking. Such thinking will be required because disparities between price and value are always accompanied by rationalizations "explaining" the discrepancy. The greater the discrepancy, the more widely believed, and thus more intimidating, the rationalization.

All right then, what *is* a stock worth? This is the conventional way to phrase the question, but I believe that it obscures the main point. The better question is this: What is the *company* worth compared to what it is selling for? To ascertain this is relatively simple, so I am flabbergasted how very few people, including investment professionals, ever get around to making the calculation. From the price of a company's stock one can easily calculate the company's "market capitalization." It is the price of a share times the number of shares outstanding. A company with ten million shares of stock outstanding, each one selling for $1, has a market capitalization of $10 million. A company with one million shares outstanding, each one selling for $10, has the same market capitalization (and thus is accorded exactly the same value by investors), even though its stock is selling for ten times as much. The difference in price per share, and other statistics figured on a per-share basis without taking into consideration the number of shares outstanding, will sometimes obscure significant distortions in value. A trendy new company with no proven track record may be ludicrously overvalued, and that fact may be concealed because its price *per share* is low.

One way of comparing the prices investors assign to comparable values is to look at the price/earnings ratio (P/E) of various stocks. The P/E is the price per share divided by a company's annual earnings per share. If a stock is selling for $50 and the company is earning $5 per share, the stock's P/E is 10.

If all companies were equally promising, all stocks would sell at the same P/E ratio. Earnings per share, after all, are a fairly objective measurement of the return one can expect from a stock. Some of those earnings are paid out in dividends. Some of them are reinvested in the company, increasing the value of its assets and its potential for future earnings.

Companies whose prospects are highly regarded by investors, however, sell for higher P/E ratios than other companies. To associate your capital with highly regarded enterprises, you must accept relatively unfavorable terms to persuade the current holders of the securities to give up their shares in what promise to be successful ventures. Shortly after the stock of Apple Computer went on sale a few years ago, the public was so enamored of its potential that it sold at a P/E of 150. In 1985 the stock of a company called Cardio Pet, which performs electrocardiograms on dogs, was selling at a P/E of 200. As in the case of Apple, investors were extremely bullish on the company's future. (An *average* P/E in 1985 was about 10.)

Occasionally, such investor confidence is justified, but more often it is not. Apple was and is a fine company, but, at a P/E of 150, the price of its stock was definitely inflated. (It later fell precipitously.) Nevertheless, investors are prone to climb on some bandwagon or another and to pay unreasonable prices for whatever stocks are the darlings of the moment. These fads usually have their origin in some genuinely shrewd observation about the worth of a particular type of security. That observation (e.g., "computer stocks are the wave of future") is gradually understood by more and more people; they act on it by buying the stocks in question, and this rewards those who first saw and acted on the insight. Eventually, everybody and his uncle is shrieking after the stocks, bidding them up way past their original underpriced state and carelessly applying the original observation to all similar-looking stocks without discrimination. Eventually, of course, the boomlet collapses.

These bandwagons do create solid investment opportunities, however. As they go tearing through the market, the stocks they leave behind, the stocks that are unfashionable at the moment, may be very good bargains indeed. In 1984, for example, a number of oil company stocks could have been purchased at a price per share that was actually less than the per-share market value of their proven oil and gas reserves (minus long-term debt). The diligent investigator can almost always find a selection of unfashionable stocks selling at low P/E ratios, and even some selling for less than "book value" (the per-share value of the company's net worth).

Of course, such statistically cheap stocks may be cheap

for a good reason (and so not really be cheap at all). Apparent bargains must be carefully investigated to see if their low prices reflect major problems. It is just as likely, however, that they have been unfairly underpriced by a trendy market that is chasing its current trend elsewhere. The drawback here is that that trend may continue for a long time. When you buy the underpriced stock of an unjustly overlooked company, you must be prepared to sit and hold your stock until other investors come to their senses and recognize its value. (Your wait may be shorter nowadays than in the past because of the emergence of corporate "raiders," who seek out underpriced companies and try to buy them out. If a single corporate raider recognizes the value of your stock and makes a takeover bid, the price of your shares may increase substantially overnight.)

Until the last few years, one place to look for underpriced stocks was among the low-priced shares of small companies. The huge pension funds and other institutional investors who play a major role in the market devoted most of their attention to the "nifty fifty" (fifty or so well-established, high-profile companies) and tended to ignore the rest. The stocks of the rest, however, tended to outperform the nifty fifty, and eventually the institutional investors caught on. They shifted their attention to the "nifty fifth," the stocks in the bottom fifth (pricewise) of those listed on the New York Stock Exchange. The inpouring of the institutions' money then created price distortions in the opposite direction. Suddenly the shares of obscure small companies were selling for relatively higher prices than those of major corporations, for no fundamentally sound reason. Shrewd investors kept an eye on the situation and watched for bargains where they could find them. Occasionally a crowd of big buyers would rush into a small company's stock on the basis of glowing predictions of future earnings. The price would soar. Then an actual earnings report would be issued that fell short of the predictions. It would not necessarily be *bad* news, just disappointing news compared to what had been expected. Major holders would sell the stock in droves. The price would dive. What had been overpriced days before was now underpriced. Observant investors moved in and picked up a bargain.

THE BLUE-CHIP OPTION

Finding underpriced stocks is, of course, easier said than done. It's one thing to master some principles of analysis; it's another to leap into the universe of ten thousand or so stocks and start sorting through financial data and making decisions.

Your broker should help you here. Backed by research department reports, he or she may in fact give you all the help you need to select stocks that are truly good values.

But the final decisions to buy will still be up to you. You may enjoy making these decisions, or the process may give you a permanent stomach ache. If you are in the latter camp, you have a couple of other good options.

One of these is to concentrate your investments in "blue-chip" stocks. These are the most visible stocks on Wall Street, issued by well-known large corporations with long records of success—General Electric, IBM, General Motors, Exxon, Sears, Du Pont . . . you get the idea. In the past, certain people confined their investments to these companies for no well-thought-out reason, but just because blue-chip stocks seemed to represent the stuff of

wisdom, forbearance, morality, and, above all, good breed-
ing. No rude little upstart companies for these investors.
They bought their ten thousand shares of General Electric
and then departed on their six-month world cruises with no
intention of interrupting their relaxations for anything so
vulgar as checking a stock price.

But there is some method to this madness. Blue-chip
companies are so large, so well established, so enmeshed
in the American economy that they are almost certain to
continue to prosper as long as America does. They may
falter, but it is unlikely that they will fall. It is more likely
that they will continue to dominate their industries because they *have* dominated them. Consumers are accustomed to buying the brands they produce. Their reputations
attract a steady stream of young talent. Their top executives are well tested in the marketplace. Because of their
sheer size, these companies attract substantial amounts of
journalistic and governmental scrutiny; they can't help but
be honest.

Investing in blue-chip stocks is certainly no way to get
rich quick. Unlike new, small, hungry companies, the
blue-chip giants are too big, and generally too conservative, to make daring moves that might double or triple the
price of their stocks in a year or two. But the very inertia
that limits the possibility of spectacular growth is a product of the momentum that almost guarantees continued
moderate growth. And steady moderate growth year after
year—say at the average historical rate of 10 percent—is
enough to make you wealthy over the course of your
long-term investment program.

If this sounds just *too* boring, there is one wrinkle to the
blue-chip strategy you might want to try. Concentrate on
the thirty stocks in the Dow Jones Industrial Average, and

keep track of their P/E ratios. These indicate which of the stocks are currently most favored by investors and which are least favored. History has demonstrated that the Dow Jones thirty periodically rotate through this in-favor, out-of-favor cycle; this year's darling was last year's dog. So it might make sense to buy the lowest P/E stocks on the list, hold them until they rise, then sell them and buy whichever Dow stocks have replaced them at the bottom of the list. There is no guarantee that every low P/E stock in the group will rise, of course, but the past is on your side here, and it is, at least, unlikely that the company will go belly-up while you are waiting for history to repeat itself.

MUTUAL FUNDS

A second way to invest in the stock market while avoiding the agonies of decision-making almost entirely is to buy shares in a mutual fund. Common-stock mutual funds, which purchase the shares of many companies and then sell shares in their own portfolios to the public, are the granddaddies of all mutual funds. They offer several advantages over individual investing:

- Mutual fund portfolios are assembled by professionals, backed by large and well-equipped research departments. You don't have to investigate companies or keep track of stock prices. They do it for you.
- Because mutual fund portfolios are well diversified, your risk is diminished. A single stock may go through the floor; it is unlikely that fifty will.
- Mutual funds are convenient. They take care of most of your bookkeeping for you, and they will be happy to

arrange for you to make an automatic monthly investment or to reinvest your dividends automatically.

For taking care of business, mutual funds charge a small
annual management fee. Some funds also charge a not-so-
small initial sales fee. This "load," which can be as much
as 8.5 percent, generally goes to the people who sell the
funds to investors. "No-load" funds, which are generally
sold via direct mail and toll-free telephone numbers, charge
no sales fees and, as a group, perform no better or worse
than load funds.

The performance of mutual funds naturally varies from
fund to fund and from year to year. A recent mediocre
year for most funds was 1986, when the value of the
average fund rose 13.4 percent while the Standard & Poor
index of 500 stocks rose 18.7 percent. You could have
done better than the average mutual fund in 1986 if you
had chosen your stocks with darts. Over the *decade* ending in 1986, however, the average mutual fund substantially outperformed a random portfolio. From 1976 through
1986, mutual funds were up 302 percent, while the S & P
500 were up 266 percent. And the longer-term record for
funds has also been good. An investor who put $10,000
into a typical mutual fund in 1956 would have had almost
$80,000 in 1980.

Even in a mediocre year like 1986, some funds performed brilliantly. (The best performance of the year was a
gain of 95 percent; the worst was a 31 percent decline.)
Much of the difference in mutual funds' performances is
attributable to differences in the philosophies that guide
fund managers in their selection of stocks. Here you must,
after all, make a choice. Some funds seek out stocks that
pay high dividends. Others seek stocks with the potential
for long-term growth. Still others aim for a compromise

combination of income and growth. Some funds specialize in the stocks of small, high-risk companies with lots of potential. Others seek stocks that are fundamentally good values but seem to be underpriced in the current market. There are funds that specialize in the stocks of gold-mining companies, or foreign companies in general. Each fund's philosophy is spelled out in a prospectus. You should read prospectuses carefully and pick a fund that shares your investment philosophy and goals—and your tolerance for risk. You might, in addition, want to look for a fund that is part of a "family" of mutual funds with different investment philosophies. Often you are allowed to switch your money freely from fund to fund (even to a money market mutual fund) as market conditions change and you change your guess about which investment philosophy is about to be rewarded.

You will also want to check a fund's past performance, of course. But keep in mind that past performance is no guarantee of future results. Many funds do well for several years and then, as market trends or the economy turn against the kind of stock they specialize in, take a down-ward turn to several years in the cellar.

HOPE, BOREDOM, GREED, AND FEAR

Whether you select individual stocks or a mutual fund, you should be buying securities that you intend to own for a long time. Remember, you are *investing*, not trading pieces of paper in search of a profit. You are not looking for stocks that will double in price in seven days but for stocks that will double in price in seven years. You are seeking out companies that are well equipped and positioned to create wealth well into the future, and you should intend to stick it out with them.

This is the kind of resolution, however, that is easier to honor in theory than in practice. Working against your resolve to buy worthy stocks and to hold them will be some very formidable enemies—hope, boredom, greed, and fear. They have undone better people than you.

Hope will encourage you to hold on to a stock when you have made a serious mistake. (Your *general* rule should be to hold stocks for a long time, but this rule should not be carved in stone. Sometimes major changes in the market or the economy mean you should abandon a position. More about this in Chapter 10.) Hope will entice you into adopting the Lighter-Than-Air Syndrome—the belief that what goes down must come back up. It ain't necessarily so. You must be ruthlessly objective with yourself and try to determine whether you are hanging on to a loser because the company is fundamentally sound, or because of the siren song of hope.

Boredom will entice you into selling stocks that you *know* are fundamentally sound but are just so . . . dull. Even a stock that is going from $10 to $100 in five years is certain to spend many days, weeks, or months doing nothing much at all. Its upward moves will tend to come in exhilarating spurts; the long periods in between may bore you to death. It is very tempting to sell out a successful but dull investment to get aboard something more exciting. Your desire to do so will, of course, be accompanied by elaborate rationalizations explaining why your successful but boring stock has really reached its peak and why its more exciting competitor is really a fabulous buy. Beware: This rationalization may be encouraged even by a sincere and honest stockbroker who has been having a slow day and needs a trade.

Greed and fear, the most powerful emotions you will encounter, are children of the great "bull" and "bear" markets that periodically sweep through Wall Street in cycles that are, to say the least, imperfectly understood. A bull market occurs when stocks go up and up and up. Everybody is making money. Everybody is happy. A bear market, conversely, is when stocks go down and down, and everybody is unhappy except the "bears," who have "sold short" or otherwise arranged their affairs to profit from a declining market. (More about these strategies in Chapter 9.)

When a bull market first begins, it is generally not recognized. When, eventually, it *is* recognized, its cause is rarely clear. As it builds, people find reasons to explain it. The longer the bull market lasts, the clearer those explanations become until, finally, everybody "knows" why the boom began and, moreover, why it is certain to continue for a good long time. This moment of clarity usually occurs immediately before the bull market collapses.

Participating in a bull market is something like eating a pizza. You wait a long time for it to arrive. When it first comes it is too hot to touch. Then you get in some good bites, but, before you are finished, it cools down and loses its appeal.

During the tastiest part of a bull market, stock prices soar to dizzying heights, carried along by their own momentum. People who wouldn't have paid $10 a share for a stock three months before will stand in line to buy it for $20. Has the fundamental value of the company changed? Almost certainly not. Only the market has changed. And people are getting greedy. They are buying stocks because stocks are going up. What they buy today for $20 they will sell next week for $22. And why not? The price went up $2 *last* week, didn't it?

Even those wise enough to see that the emperor has no clothes may go along for the ride. They are operating on the "Greater Fool Theory." They know darn well that National Slide Rule is ludicrously overpriced at $20 a share, but they expect they can sell it to some greater fool at an even more ludicrous price in a few days.

Your overriding objective in a roaring bull market is to avoid becoming the Greatest Fool at the end of the line. When everything you touch is turning to gold, when you are confident that stock prices will continue to soar, when your barber starts to congratulate you on your latest triumphs, whisper these words to yourself—"I really don't know what I'm doing. I am not a genius"—and get out.

Inevitably, the market will turn. Success will turn to dullness, then dullness will turn to disappointment. You may take to having a martini as you pick up the evening paper and review the diminution of your wealth. As the bear market gains momentum, additional drinks may become useful in putting the whole unpleasant business out of mind. But the drinks wear off by 3 A.M., when you are alone with your fears. The market is tumbling. You have lost all your paper profits. The market tumbles still. Will you lose *everything*? Out of moments like these come decisions to sell stocks at rock-bottom prices.

These panicky sellouts are major mistakes. If you have selected a stock with care, then you should not be concerned if its price is down. You bought it to hold it, so hold it. What you should be doing, in fact, during a plummeting market is not selling but *buying*. Value often increases as prices decline. If you bought a stock at $20, and it was a good buy at that price, then it is a much better buy at $10. The legendary investor Bernard Baruch made a point of stepping up his purchases of stocks he liked when their prices went down, and the practice contributed to his fortune. Dean Witter, during the depths of the Depression, advised clients, "Buy now. The present offers splendid opportunities." You too can pick up excellent bargains by taking advantage of the despair of demoralized investors—if you can only avoid the all-too-human tendency to panic along with everybody else and become one of the demoralized investors yourself.

CHAPTER 7

REAL ESTATE

PROS AND CONS

One of my colleagues at Coldwell Banker, our real estate affiliate, likes to tell a story about the engineers. The engineers are employees of a major corporation for which Coldwell Banker provides relocation services. When these engineers are transferred from one technical job to another in a distant city, Coldwell Banker helps them hunt for houses in the new location. The engineers go to great lengths to compare the various houses they are shown. First, they calculate the square footage versus the price, to arrive at the cost per square foot. Then they investigate heating and cooling costs, and break *those* down into costs per square foot. Then they painstakingly inspect the houses for defects, visible and invisible. Then they walk through the rooms with a light meter, to see how much sun shines in. Then they feed all this data into spreadsheet programs on their personal computers and generate sheafs of printouts.

Then they buy the house they have a good feeling about.

"Usually they just throw away their computer printouts so the numbers won't embarrass them," says my colleague. "Sometimes they *pretend* they've made their decision on the basis of their spreadsheets. But it just ain't so. They end up buying on pure emotion."

The decision to buy real estate—for personal use, for investment, or both—is often colored by emotional considerations. If you are buying a house, which will be by far the most expensive thing that you will ever buy, you ought to proceed fairly logically. But you may find it difficult to do so, because owning one's own home has a special significance for most Americans that transcends dollars and cents. If you are buying real estate as an investment alternative to stocks and bonds, it might be a very sound decision, but it is also likely to be influenced by myths about the inevitability of making a fortune in real estate, myths that flowered during the now-ended go-go years of the 1970s.

Home ownership and/or real estate investing may very well make sense for you, but before you fall in love with that shabby but charming Victorian at the edge of the inner city, or decide to make a million dollars fast with your own mini-empire of buildings and land, there are a few facts you ought to consider. And you must remember this:

There is nothing magical about real estate. If Santa Claus does not live on Wall Street, neither does he live in that potential turnaround neighborhood under the elevated expressway.

Everybody knows about the poor Indians who sold Man-

hattan island to the Dutch for a measly $24 in 1626. The
Dutch, it would seem, thus made the greatest real estate
investment of all time. Today, the land of Manhattan
(excluding all the buildings there, which were not part of
the original investment) is worth many billions of dollars.
Poor gullible Indians. But what if the Indians had invested
their $24 at 10 percent compound interest in 1626? By
1986, it would have grown to $17 quadrillion and change,
and the Indians, not the Dutch, would be laughing all the
way to the bank.

The Indians, of course, had no place to get such a rate
of return. But you do. And so you must compare the
potential return from a real estate investment to the returns available to you elsewhere.

Historically, real estate prices have moved up more or
less in tandem with inflation, which is somewhat reassur-
ing but hardly spectacular. Real estate investors have often earned a return significantly better than the inflation
rate by developing their properties—constructing or reno-
vating buildings. Real estate investors have also earned
handsome returns by taking advantage of tax breaks and
"leverage," both of which will be discussed in this chapter. If the real estate you purchase is your own home,
your return will be augmented as well by the opportunity
you have to live in your investment. You cannot live in a
corporate bond.

But money can also be lost in real estate. When you
own a piece of land or other property that you do not
develop with *additional* investment dollars, you are not
participating in the wealth-creation process, as you would
be if you had purchased shares of stock instead. Your
property is just sitting there. Whether or not it will increase in value depends largely on circumstances beyond
your control. Neighborhoods boom and neighborhoods de-

cay. While you are waiting to see which will happen to the neighborhood in question, your property will be costing you money—taxes, interest on the money you borrowed to buy the property, and the dividend or interest income you *could* have had if you had invested in something else instead. If the value of your property quadruples in twenty years, great. But you could have gotten the same rate of return in a certificate of deposit. (An investment quadruples in twenty years at a compound interest rate of 7.2 percent.) On the other hand (and there are some spectacular other hands in real estate), your property could just be in the path of the future development of Disney World IV. . . .

THE APPEAL OF HOME OWNERSHIP

But, first, let's talk about the quintessential American dream—home ownership.

Buying a house (or some other type of home) is the only real estate transaction most people will ever make, and it is the real estate transaction that will be most on their minds even if they never buy anything at all.

Would you like to own your own home? Or would you prefer to rent for the rest of your life? If you are a normal, red-blooded American, your answer will be loud and clear. Home ownership is part of the American dream, the part where the kids are playing outside in the yard with the white picket fence, where you are relaxing in your own living room without hearing a neighbor's stereo blaring the Sex Pistols through the floor, and out back there's a little patch of garden where any year now you're going to get around to putting in some roses.

This is what we aspire to even when, in strict financial terms, we might be better off renting. It's true that rent payments disappear forever into your landlord's pocket and do not build up your equity (ownership share) in the property you inhabit, as payments on a home mortgage do. But it's also true that the rent you pay on an apartment or house is likely to be considerably lower than the monthly cost of owning the place, which includes not only mortgage payments but also taxes, utility bills, insurance, repairs, and maintenance. The money you save can be invested in something other than a house and quite possibly earn you a rate of return equal to or better than an investment in a house. Even the widely publicized tax advantages of home ownership may or may not put you ahead of the game. The interest share of your mortgage payments (which, in the early years of a mortgage, is the largest portion of those payments) is deductible on your federal income tax return, as are local property taxes. But exactly what those deductions are worth to you will vary according to your tax bracket and other circumstances. If you don't have many other tax-deductible expenses, then the saving power of your homeowner deductions will be reduced by the standard deduction ($5,000 for a couple filing jointly, as of 1988) to which you are automatically entitled anyway. Computing the net after-tax cost of all home ownership expenses compared to the cost of renting is a calculation you ought to make—unless you're sure you don't care what the answer is because you want to own your own home and that's that. If that's the case, so be it . . . and welcome to the club.

HOUSE SHOPPING

Having decided to buy a home—either because of or despite what the figures show—you should still endeavor to keep a grip on yourself as you shop. You may well believe that you are buying a home to live in forever, and that your own likes and dislikes should therefore be the only factors in selecting one. But the odds are good that you are wrong about the forever part. Americans move a lot. They change jobs, get transferred, get divorced, get bored. It could happen to you.

When you look at a house, therefore, you should consider it not only as something you are buying but also as something you might someday be selling. It may be hard to keep this in mind when you walk through the door of an old stone house and fall in love. This happens all the time. Real estate brokers talk about houses being sold from the instant the car carrying the smitten buyer first pulls into view of the property. There is nothing silly about this. People want to feel good about the places where they live, and a lot of that feeling derives from physical appearance and from other intangible factors that people couldn't explain if they tried.

But you should also check the plumbing. And you should make a careful inquiry into the local real estate market. Your broker, if you ask, should be able to supply you with information on "comparables," homes similar to the one you are considering that have recently been sold in the area. This valuable information generally includes selling prices (and how they compare to original asking prices) and the length of time each home was on the market before it was sold. This data will tell you what types of homes—in terms of style, location, building size, and lot size—sell best in the area. It should also, it would seem, pretty much dictate the price for any home you are considering. But some sellers, especially those who have just put their homes on the market, may not yet have gotten the message that they are asking too much. Armed with your "comparable" data, you will not go along with their mistake.

In addition to supplying you with market information, your broker should ideally have personal experience in the community in which you are looking. A broker operating from an office two towns away may be eager to sell you something, but he or she is unlikely to be as helpful as one who works all the time in your target area. It is also to your benefit, on the other hand, to work with a broker who has some sort of affiliation with real estate offices in other nearby communities. Many househunters key in at the beginning of their search on a particularly well-known or desirable town in the area in which they want to live. The prices in such communities naturally reflect their popularity; frustration and disappointment ensue as shoppers learn that they cannot afford even the meanest bungalow in Beverly Hills. At this point the names of other nearby towns may be mentioned; you will be ill served by a broker who only sneers, "Oh, you wouldn't want to live *there*!" An enterprising broker with out-of-town affiliates can and should steer you to nearby communities that may be less prestigious, or a few miles inland from the beach, or a few stations farther out on the commuter line, but where perfectly fine homes are available at lower prices. As a buyer, you should bow to financial realities and be flexible.

You may also have to be flexible in the *type* of home you buy. Over the last decade, the prices of single-family houses have well outpaced the average rise in personal income. It is a sad fact that a smaller percentage of American families today can afford single-family houses than could ten, twenty, or even thirty years ago. (Even if *you* think you can swing the payments on the house you want, your bank may not agree; most financial institutions will not make a mortgage loan to anyone whose projected housing expenses exceed 28 percent of his or her income.) Real estate developers have responded to these economic facts by offering other types of housing, including cooperative and condominium apartments and semiattached houses sold on a condominium basis. Owning a condominium is very similar to owning a house. (And, in some ways, it is simpler, because exterior maintenance is usually taken care of by the condominium association.) Owning a cooperative apartment is more complicated, because co-op "owners" technically own not their apartments but shares of stock in the corporation that owns the building. Condominiums, cooperatives . . . you should investigate all the housing alternatives that you can afford. Many people who marched into real estate offices announcing, "Now don't try to show me any of those townhouse things," have been pleasantly surprised when necessity led them to consider such developments.

If you *are* able to afford a house, keep in mind the old real estate dictum that you should buy the worst house in the best neighborhood you can afford. This does not necessarily mean that you should buy a henhouse behind a mansion (although that might not be too bad an idea); it does mean that a three-bedroom house in a neighborhood of five-bedroom houses will be worth relatively more and hold its value better than a five-bedroom house in a neighborhood of three-bedroom houses.

Sometimes the owners of much-improved houses learn this lesson to their despair. They purchased a three-bedroom house in a neighborhood of three-bedroom houses. Then they added a new bedroom wing, and a swimming pool, and parquet floors, and track lighting, and a wet bar, and a hot tub. They expect to get all their money back, and maybe even more, when they go to sell.

But that's not the way the real estate market works. Some improvements, such as extra rooms, do add value to a house, although even extra rooms may add less than expected if the house has become "overbuilt" compared to its neighbors. "Lifestyle" improvements—parquet floors and the rest—rarely add as much to the selling price as they cost. A prospective buyer may loathe parquet or have a pathological fear of his dog drowning in a hot tub. Even buyers who like the improvements will see the house primarily as a three-bedroom, two-bath (or whatever) and will be unwilling to pay much more for it than they would pay for any other three-bedroom, two-bath. This fact of real estate life often makes preexisting homes better bargains than brand-new homes, because everyone who lives in a house adds *something* to it; buyers of used homes get that something—landscaping, carpeting, whatever—at a discount.

After all your looking around, you may find that you like a house that has something "wrong" with it, as reflected by prices in that real estate market. Maybe it's a colonial in a town where ranches are popular, or it's far from schools (but you don't have kids), or it has low ceilings (but you're five feet tall). Go ahead and buy it—but be sure the price is cut to reflect those faults. Even if they don't seem like faults to you, they will to somebody else. You can't count on finding a childless dwarf to sell to when you move on.

MORTGAGES

Once you have found the home you want, your shopping is still not done. It is time to shop for a mortgage.

Once upon a time, this was relatively simple. You stopped in at a couple of banks or savings and loan associations and asked what their current mortgage rates were. You picked the lowest one and signed up for a fixed-rate loan, typically for a term of thirty years. Over all that time, the interest rate would never change, nor would the amount of your monthly payment. Slowly, you built up equity in your home. At the end of thirty years, you made the last payment and burned the mortgage.

But that was before the late 1970s and the impact of double-digit inflation. Around that time, many financial institutions became very unhappy about the fixed-rate mortgage loans they had made years before. Interest rates were shooting to record highs, increasing the cost of the money these institutions borrowed from their depositors. Meanwhile, they were collecting only 6 percent interest (or less) on mortgage loans they had made during the 1960s and before. This was a bonanza for the holders of the loans, but it threatened hundreds of financial institutions— particularly savings and loan associations—with failure.

The financial institutions decided that this was no fun, so they started to push adjustable-rate mortgages on their new loan customers. These were mortgage loans on which the interest rates (and thus the monthly payments) would fluctuate with current money market interest rates. If you had an adjustable-rate mortgage and the cost of the bank's money went up, then the cost of your money would darn well go up too (within certain limits). Financial institutions thought it was only fair to share (or, from a less charitable perspective, to pass on) the risks of the volatile money market with their customers.[1]

When interest rates came back down in the 1980s, many financial institutions began to offer borrowers a choice. Today you can have a fixed-rate mortgage if you like, or you can have, at a lower rate (at least to begin), an adjustable-rate mortgage. And some institutions offer still more choices; you can select exactly what kind of adjustable-rate mortgage you like. These choices involve "caps" and "indexes." Caps are the maximum amounts that interest rates or monthly payments can be raised (or lowered) in a given period or over the life of the loan. Indexes are the areas of the money market to which interest rate increases or decreases are linked; typically the mortgage interest rate will be adjusted to remain one to three points higher than the designated index.

In 1985, one California savings and loan association was offering borrowers a choice of four different adjustable-rate loans. One plan offered fixed monthly payments for the first year, after which payments would be adjusted annually. The interest rate, however, was adjusted monthly after the first six months, so the proportion of each monthly payment dedicated to interest as opposed to repaying principal (the original amount of the loan) would vary even while the size of the monthly payment did not. The "payment cap" (the maximum amount monthly payments could move up or down at each annual adjustment) was 7.5 percent. The "rate cap" (the maximum amount the interest rate could move up or down over the entire life of

---

[1] This period of rising mortgage interest rates illustrated, once again, that there is no such thing as a free lunch. The same consumers who complained bitterly about high mortgage rates were extremely pleased to be earning high interest rates on their savings. Of course, one high rate was connected to the other.

the mortgage) was 5 percent. The index to which the interest rate was pegged was the average cost of funds for savings and loan associations in the California region as reported by the San Francisco branch of the Federal Home Loan Bank.

The second plan had identical caps, but the initial monthly payment could not change for three years. The third plan was like the first, only the interest rate was indexed to the weekly average yield on U.S. Treasury securities, an index that tends to move up or down more sharply than the Federal Home Loan Bank index. The fourth plan adjusted the loan interest rate and monthly payments every six months. The interest rate, indexed to Treasury securities, could move up or down no more than 1.5 percent a year or 4 percent over the life of the mortgage.

Is all that perfectly clear?

There's no need to get all those details straight. What is significant is that the opening interest rates charged by the institution for the various plans varied according to the institution's estimation of how well each plan protected it in the event that interest rates shot up.

Adjustable-rate mortgages often come with a below-market "teaser" rate, guaranteed for the first year or two. Even without a teaser, the rates on adjustable loans are always lower than rates on fixed loans, for the obvious reason that adjustable-loan rates need not stay that way. One New York mortgage banker in 1987 was offering a fixed-rate mortgage at 10.5 percent and an adjustable-rate mortgage at an initial rate of 7.5 percent with a 5 percent lifetime interest rate cap. So which was the better choice—the fixed-rate mortgage that would be 10.5 percent forever or the 7.5 percent adjustable-rate mortgage that might go up to 12.5 percent?

Clearly, the choice between alternative mortgages requires some calculations, some thought, and, finally, a guess about the future direction of interest rates. Younger people in the early stages of their careers might choose to go with the adjustable rate. The low initial rate may enable them to qualify for a loan on a more expensive home than they could otherwise afford, and they have reason to expect that, while interest rates may go up, so will their incomes. Borrowers who expect to be in their homes for only a few years also favor adjustable loans; they may be long gone before the rates have time to climb. Borrowers on fixed incomes, on the other hand, feel more secure with fixed-rate loans. They may not be getting a bargain, but they won't be getting any unpleasant surprises either.

Holders of fixed-rate mortgages often have the option, moreover, of refinancing their homes if interest rates drop. Just as corporations call in 15 percent bonds when rates dip to 10 percent (and then issue new bonds at the lower rate), so may holders of fixed-rate loans pay off their old mortgages with money from new, lower-interest mortgage loans. Refinancing is not cost-effective in every case, however. Mortgage lenders often charge up-front "points" (a "loan origination fee" that is actually a sort of prepaid interest) for making a new loan, and borrowers are subject to a variety of "closing costs" (lawyer's fee, appraisal fee, etc.) upon taking out a mortgage. All these costs must be balanced against the savings of having a loan at a lower rate.

Like adjustable-rate mortgages, fixed-rate mortgages also come in a variety of forms today. Among the most interesting are those in which the monthly payments increase over the term of the loan. One of these is known as the building equity mortgage, or growing equity mortgage. Initial payments are based on a thirty-year loan, but payments increase annually at a rate of 3 to 5 percent. For people with growing incomes, this is no great hardship, and the reward is substantial. The increased payments are applied directly to the outstanding principal, so the loan is paid off rapidly. With a 3 percent annual payment increase, a thirty-year mortgage will be paid off in less than fourteen years. An early payoff saves many thousands of dollars in interest payments. (Over the life of a mortgage, the amount paid in interest dwarfs the principal. Total payments on a thirty-year, $100,000 loan at 10 percent are $315,926.) On the other hand, paying off a mortgage at an accelerated rate (and accelerated payments may be made voluntarily on almost any mortgage loan) will increase the amount of your money that is tied up in the house and thus unavailable for other uses. It also decreases your "leverage"; if you sell the house any profit you make will be a lower percentage of your investment.

There are other graduated payment mortgages that do not pay off early. They start with low monthly payments that gradually rise, but they never rise high enough to pay off the mortgage before its full term. Such mortgages are suitable for borrowers who expect their incomes to increase and who qualify, on the basis of the low initial monthly payment, for houses they could not otherwise afford. But such mortgages, in their early years, often feature "negative amortization" (as do some adjustable-rate mortgages whose monthly payments are not allowed to rise fast enough to keep up with rising interest rates). "Negative amortization" means that one's monthly payments are lower than the monthly interest charges, so the unpaid balance on the loan actually grows larger month after month, even though payments are being made. The borrowers are running and running, but they keep getting farther behind. If real estate prices are booming, negative amortization may be nothing to worry about, as a house can always be sold for its increased value (or a new loan taken out against that increased value) and the loan balance paid off. If property values are level, however, negative amortization can be dangerous. A borrower may sell his home for exactly what he paid for it (or even more) and find that he still owes the bank money.

In shopping for a mortgage loan today, you will find not only many new types of mortgages, but new types of mortgage lenders as well. Banks and savings and loan associations have been joined by independent mortgage bankers, who make loans and then sell them to banks, pension funds, insurance companies, and other institutions that want to invest in mortgages. Mortgage bankers often offer loans at slightly lower rates than their competitors. You will also find some variation in the rates offered by competing traditional mortgage lenders, depending upon which institutions happen to have a surplus of lendable money on hand in a given month. Shop around—and be sure to pay attention to "points" and closing costs as well as stated interest rates. Your real estate broker should be able to advise you about mortgage lenders in the area; some real estate brokers today are even affiliated with financial institutions that make mortgage loans. Applying for a loan in a real estate broker's office is convenient, and the loan may be a good deal, but you should still investigate the alternatives yourself.

One of your best alternatives, if you can get it, is to "assume," or take over, the existing mortgage of the person who is selling you the house. If the existing mortgage is an older, low-interest one, this can be a great deal for you (but not for the lending institution, which might object).

During the height of the credit crunch a few years ago, when mortgage rates exceeded 16 percent and sellers were having trouble finding people willing or able to borrow at those rates to buy their houses, many sellers had to take personal roles in financing the sales of their homes. Often they made loans to the buyers in the form of second mortgages. These loans were used to buy out the seller's equity in an old mortgage being assumed by the buyer, or to help the buyer come up with the down payment (generally 20 percent) required by the financial institution making a new mortgage loan, or simply to provide the buyer with a loan at a lower rate than was available elsewhere. In most cases, the seller/lender would rather have been holding cash than a second mortgage, but often the only alternative to making the loan was not to sell the house.

In such cases, if the buyer makes his or her loan payments on time, the seller/lender might find the loan to be a reasonable investment. If he is desperate for cash, he can always sell the loan to somebody else (although generally at a substantial discount). Or he can simply look forward to getting all his money back from the borrower in a few years. Most seller-financed second mortgages are written as "balloons." That is, monthly payments are set as if the mortgage had a term of twenty or thirty years, but it does not. After a much shorter time, generally two to five years, the entire balance on the loan is due in one lump sum.

There are dangers for borrowers in taking on such loans. The question is: What are you going to do when the balloon comes due? If the house has substantially appreciated in value, you have no problem. You can sell it, or refinance it at its higher value, and pay off the balloon. If the house has not appreciated in value, however, you may have nowhere to turn for the money you need, and you will lose the house—unless the lender is willing to extend the term of the loan.

Even with risks like this, however, many prospective

homeowners decide they are better off buying than waiting during periods of high interest rates. High interest
rates do, after all, discourage a substantial number of
potential home buyers. The decreased demand for homes
forces sellers to offer attractive combinations of price and
terms. When interest rates drop, the demand for homes
goes up, and prices go up with it (and normal appreciation
may have driven prices higher in the meantime as well).
The higher prices may counterbalance the savings from
the lower interest rates (especially since the interest rate
portion of one's mortgage payments is tax-deductible).

If it makes sense for you to buy a home, therefore, or
you want to buy one whether it makes sense or not, there
is no particular interest-rate environment that is necessarily better or worse in which to shop for one. The important thing to remember is that you must shop—for the right
home, for the right lender, and for the right loan. This will
take more time than accepting the first loan offered by the
first lender you meet to buy the first home you feel good
about, but you could save yourself thousands of dollars for
each hour you extend the search.

REAL ESTATE INVESTMENTS

Your own home is both an investment and not an investment. You should pick it with an eye to its future
value, but you will probably find it inconvenient to buy
and sell homes as if they were shares of stock. It is far
easier to stay put and let your home function as a sort of
automatic savings account. Every month, when you make
your mortgage payment, your equity will grow, and it will
grow even more as inflation proceeds and property values

rise. You can get that equity out of your house by borrowing against it, or you can just let it sit. It will make you feel good to know that it's there.

Beyond your home, other real estate investments beckon. Some of them are "hands-off" investments. Like stocks or bonds, you buy them and eventually sell them, and in between they make no special demands on your time or energy. Such real estate investments include limited partnerships and real estate investment trusts.

Limited Partnerships

These are real estate ventures managed by a general partner with money put up by limited partners (i.e., you). Partnership entities may purchase apartment buildings, office buildings, shopping centers, or warehouses. The partnerships' goals are to return a high cash flow to investors (from rents) as well as profits from appreciation of the properties when they are sold several years down the road. Such ventures give investors (who could not afford to buy million-dollar apartment buildings on their own) many of the advantages of owning real estate without any of the headaches of management. Of course, the general partners get a nice share of the profits for their trouble.

Real Estate Investment Trusts (REITs)

These are real estate investment companies whose shares sell on stock exchanges. They are similar to limited partnerships but offer two distinct advantages:

- Your investment in an REIT is liquid. You buy it on a stock exchange and can easily sell it on a stock exchange (although you may sell it at a loss). Once you have put your money into a limited partnership, on the other hand, it may be difficult to get it out before the partnership has run its course.

• You can buy, if you like, a single share in an REIT for a few dollars. Minimum investments in limited partnerships may be much higher.

"HANDS-ON" REAL ESTATE

And then there are "hands-on" real estate investments, which offer their own distinct advantages and disadvantages. Whether they appeal to you will depend as much on your personality as on your investment goals. If you *are* a real estate kind of person, you may find such investments especially rewarding.

Consider the case of one Andrew T. Kreig, a resident of Hartford, Connecticut, who found himself with some money to invest a few years ago. At the time, Kreig was living in a rental apartment in an old section of town. His rent was exceedingly reasonable—$150 a month—but the place was getting shabby, and he was not inclined to fix it up. When a visiting woman friend remarked about some peeling wallpaper under a leak, Kreig explained, "I live by two rules: Don't eat white bread, and no capital improvements in a rented joint."

To improve his housing situation, Kreig had the choice of breaking rule number two, renting a nicer apartment at two to three times his present rent, or buying something. Looking around his own neighborhood, which is home to many poor people but has a solid core of blue-collar families and owner-occupied homes, he found a six-apartment building offered at $53,000. He put $20,000 down (money he might otherwise have used to buy stocks) and took out a fixed-rate, twenty-year, 12.5 percent mortgage. His monthly payment is $386.23.

The building Kreig bought had been haphazardly maintained by absentee landlords for decades, which was one reason the price was so low. Kreig was aware of the building's poor condition—he'd hired an independent engineer to prepare a detailed report on it before he bought—but he knew it was structurally sound and could be improved, and he was prepared to do much of the work himself.

Kreig moved into the building and began to renovate the exterior, learning about home repair as he went (and accumulating a fine set of tax-deductible tools). A gang of teenagers whom he decided to keep out of his yard by building a fence ending up pitching in and helping him build it. Skilled carpenters who lived in the neighborhood assisted with other jobs at reduced rates. Some of Kreig's neighbors were inspired by his example to fix up their own homes, which in turn increased the value of Kreig's building.

Kreig renovated the apartments in the building one at a time, as they became vacant, and raised the rents accordingly. When he first bought the building, he was charging as little as $165 a month (plus heat) for its five-and-a-half room apartments. After renovation, the same apartments went for over $400 and were considered bargains by their new tenants.

Kreig occasionally had tenant trouble—he had to evict one woman who fell $1,500 behind in her rent—but he found that the least desirable tenants generally had such chaotic personal lives that they eventually moved out of their own accord. There was little resentment of the modest rent increases he imposed on old tenants, because the increases only followed actual improvements to the apartments, and the tenants could see Kreig himself working to make those improvements. One tenant was happy to pay $40 a month more largely to have his old pull light chains replaced by mid-twentieth-century wall switches.

Four years after he bought the place, Kreig had spent an additional $24,000, but his monthly rental income well exceeded his monthly payments on his mortgage and building improvement loans (and he had substantial tax savings as well). He had received one unsolicited offer of $95,000 for the building, and his next-door neighbor had sold his (smaller) building for $110,000. Kreig held on to his property for two more years. Then he sold out—for $160,000, and a lease in the building.

Investments like Kreig's have been profitable for many Americans. Owner-occupied two- and three-family houses are common sights in many cities. By becoming small-time landlords (albeit not so ambitious as Kreig), these owners have been able to buy houses they could not otherwise have afforded. As a rule, their rental income falls short of meeting their total building costs, but it does make a substantial contribution to them, putting the owner/landlords in the happy position of building up their equity with somebody else's money. (And when they put a new roof on, half the cost is a tax-deductible business expense.)

Investors who prefer not to be their tenants' neighbors, or who have grander things in mind, buy rental houses or small apartment buildings in which they do not live themselves. But those who do the best with such investments tend to have some things in common with owner-occupants like Kreig:

• They buy in territory they know. They live near if not in their investment properties, and they are able to select wisely because of their own hometown knowledge of which neighborhoods are solid and which are not, and which depressed neighborhoods seem to be starting to turn around. These investors supplement their general knowledge of the community by carefully inspecting many properties before they buy and knocking on doors in the neighborhoods. (Although he already lived in the neighborhood himself, Kreig called on other property owners before he bought to ask about their plans for their buildings and their experiences with tenants.)

• They are prepared to work at their investments. Even if they do not intend to fix up their properties themselves, they will take the time to supervise very carefully the workers they hire. They also tend to manage their own properties—advertising for tenants, screening potential tenants, and responding to tenant problems and complaints. They could hire a management company to do all this for them, but a management fee could eat up their entire profit.

The rewards for all this effort come from several sources:

Rental Income

Every month, while money is going out for mortgage payments, tax bills, repairs, and utilities, money is also coming in. (This assumes the owner has been successful, first, in finding tenants, and, second, in finding tenants who will actually pay their rents. Both are crucial, as there is nothing more perishable than a month's rent. Once lost, it is lost forever.) Although at first the rental income from small buildings will probably not cover the owner's expenses, in the long run it probably will, since rents tend to go up faster than the costs of owning a building (especially if the owner has a fixed-rate mortgage). In the mean-time, the owner may still show a profit on the place, because of:

Tax Breaks

Interest payments on mortgage loans (and other loans as well) are deductible on the owner's federal income tax. So are property taxes and all other expenses incurred in maintaining rental property (like Andrew Kreig's new tools). Also deductible, most significantly, is depreciation. The IRS operates on the assumption that a building, *any* building, is deteriorating and losing value. On this basis, the owner is allowed to deduct a proportional share of the building's original cost every year as a loss due to depreciation. This loss is a paper loss. Even if the building is crumbling into ruin, it's not necessarily taking any actual cash out of the owner's pocket in doing so—and it may actually be *growing* in value, depending on where it is located.

Leverage and Appreciation

"Leverage" results from the fact that most people do not buy real estate for all cash. If you buy a $100,000 property, you may put down as little as $10,000 and take a mortgage for the rest. If the property then proceeds to appreciate 15 percent a year for two years, you can sell it for $130,000. This is a profit not of 30 percent but of 300 percent on your original investment. (This is also a simplified example, as it would have cost you something to own the building for two years and to sell it; even so, leverage vastly increases your profit potential.)

But leverage can also work against you. If you go to sell your $100,000 property and find that you can get only

$100,000 for it, and you have in the meantime spent $10,000 to maintain it and bring it to market, then you have lost 100 percent of your original investment, even though your property is still worth what you paid for it. If property values have actually gone down, your situation will be catastrophic.

Property values generally go up, however, at least at the rate of inflation. During the boom real estate years of the late 1970s, when real estate values zoomed way beyond inflation, leverage and appreciation worked together to make many real estate investors rich. Typically, an investor would buy a $100,000 property, say, with a $10,000 down payment and a $90,000 mortgage. A year or so later, when the property was worth $120,000 he would take out an additional $20,000 loan against its increased value. He would use that $20,000 to make down payments on another property or two. When *their* value increased, he would repeat the process. From a single $10,000 down payment, he might end up with dozens of properties.

As long as property values roared upward, this was a very profitable game. Like all Great Truths of the past, however, the proposition that "you can't lose money buying real estate" attracted swirling mobs of adherents—and then ceased being true. Property values levelled off. Investors who didn't get off the escalator in time were hurt.

Today it is not so easy to make a fortune with $10,000 down. The real estate boom times have gone and are unlikely to return any time soon. But even modest appreciation, abetted by leverage (and the natural equity buildup that ensues simply by making one's mortgage payments), can still enable a smart and gutsy investor to borrow against one property to buy another and thus pyramid a modest real estate empire, albeit at a slower pace.

But there are no guaranteed fortunes in real estate. The

market can turn sour. Tenants can turn surly. And there are some additional drawbacks to real estate that do not apply to stocks and bonds:

- Real estate is not liquid. You can always sell a share of stock. You may not always be able to find a buyer for a building.
- The real estate selling commission is a stiff one, typically 6 percent (and 10 percent on raw land). On a $100,000 house on which you have made a 10 percent down payment, the commission can amount to a whopping 60 percent of your original investment. You have to make a pretty good profit when you sell to overcome that.
- Although depreciation may be exaggerated by the tax tables, buildings *do* fall apart. Maintenance is a constant and costly necessity and must be carefully calculated in any estimate of the rate of return on a real estate investment.

REAL ESTATE VS. THE STOCK MARKET

Historically, the typical real estate investment has yielded a return roughly comparable to the typical investment in common stocks. For most investors, real estate or the stock market is the best place to put long-term capital. But which one? To determine which type of investment would be best for *you*, ask yourself the following questions:

1. Can you tell a hammer from a ham sandwich?
Some people like to fix up buildings; others are ignorant of the process and wish to remain so. If you're in the latter

camp, real estate is probably not for you. True, there's nothing that somebody can't be hired to fix for you, but paying that somebody will eat into the rate of return on your investment.

2. When the man in the native marketplace asks 500 pesos for the wood carving of Don Quixote, do you:

    a) give him 500?
    b) offer 200 and resolve to settle for 300?
    c) get a stomach ache and go back to the hotel?

Negotiation is crucial to the process of making money in real estate. Often one's entire profit or loss on a property derives from how good a bargain one makes when one buys it. Investors in stocks and bonds don't have to deal with this situation. If General Motors is being offered at $85 a share, no one is going to offer much less than $84.75 for it. The "negotiation" will take a few seconds at most and will be handled entirely by representatives of the buyer and the seller, not the investors themselves. If a building, on the other hand, is offered for sale at $85,000, a bid of $70,000 might be entirely appropriate, and the ensuing negotiation may have as much drama as *The Perils of Pauline*.

3. Would you like a part-time job?

Maintaining and managing buildings takes time or money or both. You can hire somebody to do it for you, or you can "hire" yourself and save the money. If you are retired, semi-retired, or simply energetic, taking an active role in running your property may be a satisfying and remunerative job.

4. Do you have trouble saving money?

If you have $50,000 invested in the stock market, no one is going to come over to your house and *make* you invest still more on a regular basis. You can buy that life-size carving of Don Quixote instead. If you have $50,000 invested in a building, however, you have to make your monthly mortgage payments (thus building up your equity) or the bank will take your building away. This is a powerful incentive to keep up your investment program.

5. Are you at all prone to panic? (Come on, admit it.)

At the bottom of the Great Depression, many investors, gripped by the unreasoning panic that investors invariably feel in the depths of any great bear market, sold the stocks of essentially sound companies at ridiculously low prices. A few years later, they rued the day they had done so. Real estate investors, on the other hand, tended not to sell out at the worst possible time, not because they didn't panic but because there was nobody around to whom they *could* sell. There is almost always a buyer for shares of stock, if the price is low enough. The real estate market is "thinner"; in bad times it is hard to find any buyer at all. This makes it harder for real estate investors to make foolish mistakes.

6. Can your ego accept bad news?

If you have made a bum decision and bought a turkey of a stock, the fact will stare you in the face. Every day, that stock's current price will be printed in the newspaper, as if just for your personal torture. You bought it at $100; it is selling at $10; there it is, in black and white.

But if you buy a bum property, or a good property at an outlandish price, how do you know it? There may be no human being on earth willing to pay you anything near what you paid for that lot on Skid Row, but you won't know that for a fact unless you try to sell it. The price of your lot is not printed in the newspaper every day. True, you may hear of similar lots being sold for pathetic prices, but those reports may not be true, and you can always assure yourself that the lot next to yours that just sold for $200 was nothing at all, *really*, like your lot (the weeds were shorter). If you begin to doubt, you can always call the broker who sold you the property. He'll be happy to tell you what a great buy you made.

7. Do you like to be involved?

There is a certain satisfaction in buying a stock at $10 a share and watching it grow to $20 over the next five years, but for some people there is far greater satisfaction in locating a rundown building, negotiating its purchase, redesigning it, fixing it up, locating tenants, negotiating leases, lobbying the city council on rent control, learning about the tenants' problems, attending a tenant's son's bar mitzvah, fixing leaks, doing the books, watching the neighborhood turn around—and then doing it again.

If you would like to be this actively involved with your investments, then look to real estate. If reading the financial pages and making an occasional telephone call to your broker is activity enough for you, then stick with stocks for your long-term investments. The choice is yours.

CHAPTER 8

LIFE INSURANCE

PRINCIPLES OF INSURANCE

I recently spoke to an elderly widow who asked me to look over her financial affairs. It turned out that they were rosy. She had a net worth of more than $400,000 and living expenses of about $30,000 a year. Her assets included stocks and bonds as well as savings and checking accounts that alone contained more than $35,000.

And then there was her life insurance policy. Every year, year after year, she was paying a few hundred dollars for an old policy with a death benefit of $25,000. The cost was modest, but I could see no reason for her to be spending anything at all on life insurance. What did she need it for?

"That's to bury me," she said.

Oh. I cast my eyes down at the list of her assets. "We could sell a few shares of AT&T to bury you," I said. I glanced at her latest bank statement. "We could just write the funeral director a *check.*"

This had never occurred to her. She had the idea that her life insurance policy—and only her life insurance policy—was guaranteeing that her body would not some-day be tossed into a mass grave in a potter's field. This was "pocket accounting" in the extreme. The fact that she had accumulated enough assets to pay for a catered funeral on the moon, if she wanted one, had not changed her old way of thinking.

The purchase of life insurance, like every other financial decision, must be approached with a fresh and clear per-spective. You almost certainly *do* need life insurance, and you may well need a great deal more of it than you think. But you should understand the reasons for purchasing it as well as its real cost. In today's investment environment, any money diverted from earning the highest possible return may be costing you a great deal.

It will probably come as no surprise to you that life insurance companies are not benevolent nonprofit institu-tions (any more than are banks, brokerage houses, or real estate agencies). Nor are insurance companies reckless gamblers. In fact, they are not gamblers at all.

Insurance companies do *seem* to be gamblers, as their business is based on an endless series of bets with individ-uals as to when they will die. Policyholders who sign up, pay a premium or two, and then promptly kick the bucket "win" their bets; the company pays their beneficiaries more than the policyholder ever paid the company. Poli-cyholders who live to ripe old ages "lose" their bets; they may pay more in premiums than their heirs will ever get back. The insurance companies have a nice edge in this process, in that everyone who buys a policy works very hard to lose his or her bet with the company.

But the insurance company wins overall no matter who wins in any individual case. That's because death statistics are not random but highly predictable. It is impossible to know, of course, when Joan Blow, age thirty-six, will go to meet her maker. But assemble a pool of ten thousand thirty-six-year-old women, and actuaries, guided by years of death records, can predict with fair accuracy how many of those women will die next year, and the year after that, and so on. Because it knows, therefore, how many (not which ones, but how many) of its policyholders will die every year, it is an easy matter for an insurance company to set its rates high enough to cover all the death benefits it will have to pay and also earn a profit—barring an unforeseeable mass calamity. (Insurance companies specifically exclude death from nuclear war from coverage.)

So the insurance companies are able to make a buck and stay in business. And this is a good thing, because, by providing a mechanism for individuals to share the financial risks of premature death, they perform a valuable service. The affordable sums of money they collect from many individuals form a pool that is redistributed to families of deceased policyholders—families that would be facing financial catastrophe were it not for life insurance.

This is the prime purpose of life insurance, and the only reason most people should have life insurance—to protect one's dependents from a major decline in their standard of living if the policyholder dies before he or she has had enough time to accumulate a substantial estate. Some day, if you have the ability and discipline to adopt and maintain the kind of investment plan we have discussed in this book, you will not need life insurance. You will have achieved financial serenity, and, when you die, your dependents will be able to live nicely on the assets you leave behind. (If your assets are substantial but not liquid, you may want to retain life insurance to help your heirs pay estate taxes.)

Even if you have embarked on a steady investment program, however, you may die before you have time to reach your goal. As a young or middle-aged working person, you may still be years away from it. If you died, your family would be in trouble. Life insurance provides, at the moment of your death, an instant shortcut to the goal you did not have time to reach. You need this guarantee to protect your family, and you cannot get it from anything but life insurance. Before you begin any other kind of investment program, therefore, you must be sure that your insurance needs are met.

HOW MUCH DO YOU NEED?

What are your insurance needs?

There is no pat answer to that question. Various rules of thumb hold that a breadwinner with a family of four should have insurance equal to five to ten times his or her annual income. But every case is unique, and you can determine your own insurance needs only by making some fairly extensive calculations about your personal situation.

To begin, your family will need a lump sum to pay for your "last expenses"—funeral, medical bills not covered by health insurance, and incidentals related to your departure. Then, on an ongoing basis, your family will need in the range of 60 to 75 percent of the income you are no longer earning to maintain themselves in the style to which they are accustomed. (They will no longer need 100 percent of your income, because you will no longer be around drinking expensive imported beer and spilling ketchup on your silk jacket.) Your family will need a big boost in income (or an extra lump sum) during your children's college years, if that is where they are headed. Afterward, income needs will be less, as your children start to earn their own livings; still less money will be needed when your surviving spouse reaches retirement age and will presumably begin to receive a pension.

The first step in figuring your insurance needs is to find the sum that will provide for all your family's one-time expenses and still leave enough to generate the income they will need over the long term. That sum must be increased to allow for inflation; it may be decreased in recognition of the fact that your family can gradually dip into the principal as well as live off the interest. Any life insurance salesman (many of whom are armed nowadays with computer terminals and programs for working up these figures) will be only too pleased to help you with your calculations.

The number you come up with is likely to be $250,000 or more, but do not be alarmed. Not all of that money will have to be provided by life insurance. Depending on the size of your contributions to Social Security over the years and the number of dependents in your family, your surviving spouse and children may be eligible for Social Security benefits of up to $1,000 a month or more (although benefits may stop when your youngest child reaches age eighteen and will be cut back before that if your spouse is working). Any Social Security benefits received will reduce your need for insurance by the amount required to produce that income. Your insurance needs will also be reduced by your spouse's future income potential (although that may be offset by child-care and housekeeping costs) and possible support from doting grandparents. Finally, there is the important matter of the wealth you have already accumulated. Whatever your family will inherit from you can be deducted from the amount of insurance you need. (In the unlikely event that you have already accumulated enough, you do not need insurance at all, unless you want some to help pay estate taxes.)

Whatever your final conclusion about your insurance needs, it is important to review your calculations on a regular basis. Circumstances will change. Your son's braces will come off. Your daughter will finish college. Your investments will grow. As the years go by, your insurance needs may decrease. Or you may have triplets. Congratulations—and call your insurance agent.

It may be just as important, by the way, to have insurance on a homemaker spouse as on the family breadwinner. Full-time homemakers serve as child-care workers, housekeepers, cooks, and more. Hiring people to fill those jobs is likely to be surprisingly expensive. Insurance can provide the money to pay for it.

The need for insurance in childless couples is less obvious, but many two-income couples have financial commitments, like mortgage payments, that a surviving spouse could not handle alone. In addition, the survivor will need to pay "last expenses."

And what if you are single, with no entangling financial alliances and no dependents at present or on the horizon? You may want some insurance to spare your parents the burden of "last expenses." Beyond that, you probably do not need insurance at all. Young people are often urged to buy insurance with the argument that it is much cheaper to buy a policy at age twenty-five, say, than at age forty (for the very good reason that a twenty-five-year-old is less likely to die than a forty-year-old). But the cheapness argument can be misleading. If you are buying term insurance, on which the premium increases as you get older, you will pay the same premium at age forty as any other forty-year-old, no matter how long you have had your policy. If you are buying whole life insurance, on which the premium never changes, you will indeed be paying a lower premium than a person who takes out the policy at age forty, but you will be sacrificing the interest you could have earned by investing that money elsewhere over the life of the policy. And, even if the policy really is cheap, why buy it if you don't need it?

One good argument *for* buying insurance when young is that many companies offer policies that guarantee you the right to buy more insurance later at standard rates, even if your health has deteriorated. If you eventually acquire both dependents and health problems, this guarantee could be valuable.

YOUR INSURANCE OPTIONS

Once you have established your insurance needs, the first thing you should do is determine how much insurance you already have. Many employees get group life insurance as a fringe benefit of their jobs. If your insurance needs are modest, such a policy may be all that you require. You may also have, or be eligible to buy, inexpensive group insurance through organizations of which you are a member.

If these policies do not cover your needs, then you should buy insurance, and buy it promptly. As you begin to shop around, you will quickly encounter three main varieties:

Term Insurance

This is the cheapest kind of life insurance. As such, it is often the policy of choice for young families with large insurance needs and modest incomes.

Term insurance is "pure" insurance. Unlike whole life and universal life (described below), term insurance has no savings or investment component. You pay the insurance company an annual premium. They pay your beneficiary if you die. And that's all there is to it. If you do not die during the term of the policy, the company gets to keep all the money you have paid in (although some of that money, of course, will have been paid out to the beneficiaries of other term policyholders who "won" their bets with the company by dying).

Term insurance is often sold on an "annual renewable" basis. Every year the policy expires and you have the option of renewing. But every year the policy will be more expensive. At age twenty-five, you may pay little more than $1 for each $1,000 of coverage you get. (Women always pay less than men, because they live longer, and many companies offer special rates to nonsmokers, because *they* live longer too.) At age forty, you may pay almost $2 per $1,000. At age sixty, you may pay more than $7 per $1,000. As you enter old age, the cost of term insurance eventually becomes prohibitively high—but you may no longer need insurance by then.

Term insurance can also be purchased for longer terms, during which the annual premium will remain level. Since the actual cost of insuring you rises inexorably every year as you age, the insurance company manages to keep the premium level by overcharging you during the early years and undercharging you later on. If you renew the policy when it expires, the annual premium will then go up.

Another variation on term insurance is "decreasing term," where you pay the same premium every year, but the size of the death benefit goes down. A common variety of decreasing term is mortgage insurance, which many lenders require home buyers to purchase. The face value of the policy decreases year by year in step with the amount due on the mortgage. If the borrower dies, an amount sufficient to pay off the mortgage instantly becomes available. (Similar "credit insurance" policies are available to pay off other kinds of indebtedness.)

These policies protect the borrower's family, but they also protect the mortgage lender. If you have the option not to buy mortgage insurance, it is often a good idea to opt out. Instead of buying a separate policy earmarked for your mortgage (a clear case of "pocket accounting"), you should figure your family's housing expenses into your calculation of your total insurance needs and make sure they are covered by whatever policy you do buy. You may end up getting the equivalent of mortgage insurance at a lower rate (a $200,000 policy costs less than two $100,000 policies), and your family will have the choice of paying off the mortgage or simply continuing to make monthly payments while investing the rest of the insurance proceeds elsewhere.

Regular term policies are offered with a wide range of options. Two common and valuable ones are the automatic right of renewal up to age sixty-five or seventy, regardless of what happens to your health, and the right to convert your policy to whole life insurance, again regardless of the future state of your health.

Another potentially valuable option is known as "waiver of premium." This provides that your insurance will continue in force, with no further premium payments from you, if you become disabled.

One option you do not want is "double indemnity." This provides for a doubled death benefit if you die as a result of an accident or violence instead of disease. There is, however, no reason why your dependents' needs should be any greater if you are killed by a runaway oxcart than if you die of double pneumonia. The extra charge for double indemnity is better spent buying a slightly larger policy without that feature. Similarly, you should avoid "accidental death and dismemberment" policies unless you are planning to fall off a cliff soon. Such policies are cheap, but they pay nothing to your survivors if you die of natural causes, as most people do.

Whatever you buy, shop around. Term insurance rates vary widely from company to company. But keep in mind that whole life insurance rates vary also. A company with low term rates may have high whole life rates. That should affect your choice of company if you think you may someday want to convert your policy. You may also find, if you have any kind of medical problem, that some companies may insist on charging you extra as a result while others do not.

Whole Life Insurance

Whole life insurance is more expensive than term. Whole life is also known as "permanent" life insurance, because the coverage never expires as long as you keep paying the annual premium. Unlike term, the premium never increases; it is fixed for life when you buy the policy. (The younger you are when you buy, the lower the premium will be.) Since the premiums are held level, while the actual cost of insurance necessarily increases as you age, you are in effect overpaying during the early years of your policy. Some of that overpayment goes to build up "cash value."

The cash value of a policy gradually increases, and it will be paid to you if you cancel the insurance. (It is not added to the face value of the policy if you die, however.) It takes a number of years for the cash value to build up to a substantial sum. Once it does, you may draw on it to pay your premiums. You may also borrow it out of the policy at a low interest rate, possibly to invest it elsewhere at a higher rate for an automatic profit. You need never repay such loans, but the amount you have borrowed will be deducted from the death benefit paid to your beneficiary when you die.

There are two common variations on whole life that require you to pay premiums for only a limited number of years. With a "limited payment life" policy, you pay for a set period (usually ten years, twenty years, or until you turn sixty-five), after which the policy is "paid up" and remains in force with no additional payments. "Endowment" policies not only become paid up after a specified period but also then pay the face value of the policy to you even if you are still alive. The premiums on these policies are, not surprisingly, higher than those on comparable amounts of ordinary whole life insurance policies (and premiums on endowment policies are higher than those on limited payment life policies). You will thus be sacrificing some insurance coverage, possibly during the years you need it most, if you buy either of these.

Some whole life policies, finally, are known as "participating" policies and pay "dividends" to policyholders if the insurance company's investments (which it buys with the premium money it collects from policyholders) perform well. This enables policyholders to share some of the benefits reaped by the company during periods of high interest rates. Participating policies, however, charge higher premiums than "nonparticipating" policies to begin with.

(The IRS defines whole life dividends as refunds of "overpayments of premiums.") The payment of dividends may or may not proceed to make the participating policies cheaper.

Universal Life Insurance

For many years life insurance agents encouraged consumers to buy whole life insurance instead of term because of the savings function of the cash value buildup in whole life policies. And for many years consumers were satisfied to hand over annual premiums to insurance companies and see their cash values (possibly augmented by dividends) pile up at modest rates of return.

With the coming of money market funds and other new investment opportunities, however, those consumers who were paying attention began to notice that they could earn a much higher return on their savings elsewhere than in a whole life insurance policy. It became smart to buy term insurance and invest the difference—the amount you were saving by not buying whole life—in something more profitable.

Insurance companies have responded to these changes in the investment marketplace by introducing "universal life" which, in a sense, enables consumers to buy term and invest the difference, all within one life insurance contract.

Part of the premium paid into a universal life policy is allocated to pay for term insurance (on a permanent renewing basis). Part goes to pay maintenance and management fees and to give the insurance company its profit. The rest goes into a cash value fund, which functions as an investment. Competitive rates of return are paid on the money in that fund. Some low rate of return (typically 4 or 4.5 percent) is guaranteed; the actual rate paid will depend upon the performance of the insurance company's investments. Whatever the rate of return, no income tax is due on growth in the cash value fund until the money is paid out. (This is true of the cash value funds in whole life insurance policies as well.) This allows the money in the fund to compound tax-free—the same valuable advantage offered by IRAs and annuities.

Universal life policies offer the additional advantage of being extremely flexible. It is easy to change the amount of the death benefit, and also to increase or decrease the amount of the annual premium. You may increase the premium if you wish to build up your investment fund. You may decrease it as low as the bare minimum required to pay for your insurance coverage (an amount approximately equivalent to a term insurance premium) and maintenance fees. You may decrease the premium below that level, or even withdraw money from the policy, as long as there remains enough money in your cash value fund to cover the minimum premium.

The table opposite illustrates how this might work in practice. It documents the history of a universal life policy sold to Joe Blow at age thirty-one. Notice that it actually illustrates two possible future courses for the policy. The "guaranteed cash value" column shows what happens if the cash value fund grows only at its low guaranteed rate of 4 percent, an unlikely circumstance. The "projected cash value" column shows what happens at a return of 8.5 percent, a reasonable forecast in today's investment environment.

Joe Blow's Universal Life Policy

Year	Age	Premium Paid	Guaranteed Cash Value (4% return)	Projected Cash Value (8.5% return)	Death Benefit
1	32	$1,200	$ 313	$ 313	$212,000
2	33	1,200	1,163	1,190	212,000
3	34	1,200	2,037	2,132	212,000
4	35	1,200	2,935	3,141	212,000
5	36	1,200	3,854	4,221	212,000
6	37	1,200	4,794	5,384	212,000
7	38	1,200	5,750	6,637	212,000
8	39	1,200	6,721	7,990	212,000
9	40	1,200	7,704	9,449	212,000
10	41	1,200	8,697	11,028	212,000
11	42	1,200	9,695	12,734	212,000
12	43	1,200	10,698	14,561	212,000
13	44	5,000	15,382	20,377	212,000
14	45	1,600	16,932	23,231	212,000
15	46	1,600	18,500	26,291	212,000
16	47	1,600	20,082	29,603	212,000
17	48	1,600	21,677	33,185	212,000
18	49	1,600	23,282	37,062	212,000
19	50	1,600	24,891	41,253	212,000
20	51	1,600	26,501	45,788	212,000
21	52	withdraws 5,000	21,345	43,641	207,000
22	53	withdraws 5,000	15,883	41,281	202,000
23	54	withdraws 5,000	10,090	38,694	197,000
24	55	withdraws 5,000	3,931	35,861	192,000
25	56	2,400	4,915	40,616	192,000
26	57	2,400	5,792	45,756	192,000
27	58	2,400	6,547	51,311	192,000
28	59	2,400	7,163	57,313	192,000
29	60	2,400	7,610	63,807	192,000
30	61	2,400	7,858	70,848	192,000
31	62	2,400	7,872	78,477	192,000
32	63	2,400	7,605	86,758	192,000
33	64	2,400	6,999	95,758	192,000
34	65	2,400	5,989	105,525	192,000
35	66	2,400	4,507	116,133	192,000
36	67	withdraws 20,000	policy	103,514	172,000
37	68	withdraws 20,000	cancelled	89,809	152,000
38	69	withdraws 20,000		74,927	132,000
39	70	withdraws 20,000		58,761	112,000
40	71	withdraws 20,000		41,172	92,000
41	72	0		43,689	92,000
42	73	0		46,333	92,000
43	74	0		49,132	92,000
44	75	0		52,117	92,000

In the first year of the policy, Joe pays a premium of $100 a month, or $1,200 a year. Part of that goes to pay for $212,000 of life insurance coverage. Part goes to the insurance company to pay its costs and make its profit. And the rest, $313, goes into Joe's cash value fund. (Note that in succeeding years a much higher proportion of the premium goes into the cash value fund. The policy illustrated here draws a large portion of its total lifetime allocation for maintenance and profit from the first year's premium.)

After a few years, during which Joe continues to pay a $1,200 premium, the difference between the guaranteed and projected cash value buildups begins to increase. By the seventh year, the projected cash value column is increasing by more than the $1,200 Joe is putting into the policy. The return earned by Joe's cash value fund is sufficient to pay for Joe's insurance coverage and still have some left over.

In the thirteenth year, Joe decides to make a $5,000 lump-sum payment into the policy to beef up its investment component. Thereafter, he increases his annual premium to $1,600 for the same reason.

During years twenty-one to twenty-four, Joe stops making annual payments and instead withdraws $5,000 from the policy each year to help pay his daughter's college costs. The face value of the policy is reduced by the amount of each withdrawal (just as it would be if Joe were borrowing from the cash value of a whole life policy), but the insurance continues in force; the cost of the insurance is simply deducted from the balance in the cash value fund.

In the twenty-fifth year, Joe resumes making premium payments, at an annual rate of $2,400, and his cash value fund begins to grow again. Note, however, that after the age of sixty-two, the cash value in the 4 percent column begins to decline. Remember, Joe's account is being charged for insurance at term rates, and term insurance becomes expensive as you grow older. In this case, it is costing more than the $2,400 a year Joe is paying as a premium. The difference is being made up from the cash value fund, and the 4 percent fund is not earning enough to pay that difference and continue to grow. The 8.5 percent fund, on the other hand, *is* earning enough to make up the difference and still grow.

The 8.5 percent fund finally begins to decrease only when Joe retires and begins to withdraw $20,000 a year from his policy. After several years, to avoid depleting (and cancelling) the policy, Joe stops taking money out, but neither does he put any more money in. With no additional payments, his insurance remains in force, and a substantial amount remains (and grows) in his cash value fund.

And that's universal life. One variation now being offered by some insurance companies is universal variable life, which allows policyholders to decide how their cash value funds will be invested. In ordinary universal life, the cash value funds of all policyholders are pooled and invested as the insurance company sees fit. In the variable variety, each policyholder specifies which of several mutual funds he wants his cash value invested in; depending upon how well he chooses, his return may be higher or lower than that of other policyholders.

The competition for insurance dollars nowadays is intense, and it is not easy for consumers to select the best universal life policy. Cash values in different policies build up at different rates, varying not only with the rate of return being earned but also by how each insurance company chooses to deduct its charges for administration and profit. The best way to compare two policies is to look at their projected cash buildups—at the same projected interest rate—some years down the road.

Some companies do pay higher interest rates than others and make a great point of it in their sales promotion. The field is thick with young companies promising high rates of return. To deliver those high returns, however, the companies may be forced to invest in riskier securities than companies promising lower returns. Remember that, with universal life, you will be sharing that risk. Or the company promising a high return may be practicing a sort of "bait-and-switch" tactic. A young company with few policies on its books can afford to pay an above-market rate of return for a couple of years and absorb the loss, because it is not paying that return on very many policies. After it has attracted a load of new customers, it may slowly drop its rate of return to the level of other companies, or even below.

One thing about universal life is clear: Its competitive rates of return make it a better value than whole life insurance in most circumstances. If you already have a whole life policy, it may be in your interest to cancel it and switch to universal life. Whether this is a good move or not will depend on a number of factors, including the specifics of your current policy and your age. Some whole life policies include attractive options that you may not want to give up. If your whole life policy has been in force for a number of years, it may finally be accumulating cash value at a rapid rate. In such a case, you may be better off keeping it in force, paying the annual premium, then immediately borrowing the amount of the premium (and perhaps more) back out of the policy and using that money to buy universal life. Or you may, after all, simply be better off cancelling it. To determine your best course, you'll have to go over the details of your old policy and the proposed new one with an insurance professional. To make the hearing fair, you may want to include two insurance professionals—the one who wants to sell you universal life and the one who originally sold you the whole life policy.

INSURANCE VS. INVESTING ON YOUR OWN

Even though universal life marks an undisputed advance over the rate of return paid on whole life policies, there still remains one obvious drawback to using insurance for investment purposes. Insurance companies take the money paid in by policyholders and invest it in real estate and government and corporate securities. You can do the same thing and eliminate the middleman. By investing directly in the things insurance companies invest in, you can pocket all the proceeds yourself (minus brokerage commissions) instead of splitting them with an insurance company.

This is the basis for the traditional advice to "buy term and invest the difference." The advice makes sense if—and this is a crucial if—you really do invest the difference.

Most people who buy term insurance do not. They take the money they have saved by not buying whole life or universal life and use it for a trip to Miami Beach, or to buy a new suit, or a used car, or whatever. The most effective response insurance salesmen have when prospects tell them they only want term insurance is, "If you save as much in the next ten years as you have saved in the last ten years, will you be satisfied?" Most people must answer no, because they have not been saving or investing. Their money has been slipping through their fingers.

Cash-value life insurance has therefore been a boon to millions of Americans, because it has forced them to save in spite of themselves. They've had to pay their insurance premiums or lose the coverage they knew they needed; in the process they built up cash value in their policies. (In this, life insurance replicates the savings function of a home mortgage; homeowners must make their monthly payments, and thus build up equity in their homes, if they don't want to lose them.) The return on such insurance-driven savings (at least in whole life policies) has been low, but at least there have been savings.

Be honest with yourself. If you are unlikely to develop and maintain your own investment program, or you do not want the responsibility or cares of doing so, then you will do well to buy universal life. If you are willing and able to invest on your own initiative on a relentlessly regular basis (and you are willing to shoulder the risks involved), then you will be better off doing that than paying an insurance company to do it for you.

CHAPTER 9

SPECULATION

WHO CAN AFFORD TO SPECULATE

This chapter is about ways to lose your money. You probably don't need to read it. I'm sure you can think of plenty of ways to lose your money all on your own without any suggestions from me, and I am reluctant to put any new bad ideas into your head. Nevertheless, duty demands that we cover some of the flashier investment strategies and vehicles that are mentioned from time to time in the newspapers. These are generally described as being best suited to "sophisticated" investors, as if there were something unsophisticated about prudent, profitable, value-based' investing. ("How gauche! That man over there is drinking red wine with his fish. And *that* man is buying some high-rated corporate bonds. I can't bear to watch.") In fact, so-called sophisticated investments are really the domain of speculators.

You will recall the old risk/return trade-off: The greater the potential reward offered by an investment, the riskier the investment will be. Speculators deal at the far edge of that trade-off. They pursue investments that promise rich—and fast—payoffs. In return, they risk losing the entire amount they have invested, and sometimes more.

There is, of course, some risk associated with any investment. Any stock can run into trouble. Any neighborhood can hit the skids. And even investors in "absolutely safe" securities, like U.S. Treasury bonds, may find that their rate of return is less than the rate of inflation. There are many ways to lose.

Still, prudent investors can measure risks with some degree of accuracy. By being content with modest but profitable returns, they need live only with modest but acceptable risks. This is the kind of investment program you should have and the kind that will, over time, make you financially secure.

Speculators throw all that out the window. They want to double their money in the next three months, and they are prepared to lose their entire investment in the effort—or they ought to be prepared to do so, because that is exactly what happens to many speculative investments. Many of the greatest speculators of all time, including those who made several fortunes, died broke. Speculating is gambling, and gamblers tend to play until they lose.

It is often said that young people just starting out in their careers are in the best position to speculate, because they have the most time to recoup any losses. Conversely, the conventional wisdom holds that people at or approaching retirement should be the most cautious with their investments, as they husband their resources for old age.

To this conventional wisdom, I say baloney! Consider a twenty-five-year-old accountant and her sixty-year-old father. The twenty-five-year-old is unlikely to have much capital. She doesn't earn very much yet, and she likes to spend what she does earn. If she has saved $5,000, say, it has likely been with very great difficulty. If she takes a flyer with that $5,000 and loses it (which is the fate of most flyers), it may take her years to accumulate another investment stake, and she may be soured on the whole idea of investing, to boot. More dramatic than that, however, is the actual financial impact of what she has lost. Her $5,000, if it had been put into a conservative investment program yielding just 10 percent, would have grown to $140,512 by the time she was her father's age. Now, however, because some Bolivian gold mine did not pan out for her, she has lost not just $5,000 but also all the years of compounding and growth that $5,000 would have earned. Her speculation has been far more costly than she knew.

Her father, on the other hand, has fewer years of compounding to look forward to. His $5,000 loss would be a lot nearer to $5,000 than to $140,512. This does not mean that he should gamble with money he needs for retirement; it just means that he has less to lose than his daughter.

Both the person approaching retirement and the younger person can fairly easily calculate exactly how much money, if any, they can afford to speculate with. Consider a forty-three-year-old architect who would like to retire on $200,000 a year. (Actually, he'd be very happy to retire on $50,000 a year—if he were retiring tomorrow—but he has built some leeway into his goal to allow for future inflation.) He figures (again allowing for inflation) that his Social Security and company pension will be worth at least $40,000 a year to him when he retires, so he'll need to have annual investment income by then of $160,000. He figures that he'll be able to earn 10 percent on his capital;

that means he'll need to have a net worth of $1,600,000 when he retires.

That may sound like a lot of money, but our architect still has twenty-two years to go before retirement. If he can earn 10 percent a year on his investments between now and then, any money he has today will octuple (increase eightfold). (Once again, the miracle of compound interest: $1 invested at 10 percent per annum will grow to $8.14 in twenty-two years.) So, to achieve his lifetime investment goal, he needs a net worth right now of $200,000. He figures his net worth by drawing up a personal balance sheet, as described in Chapter 3. If he discovers that his net worth is $200,000 on the nose, then he must invest it prudently to earn no less than 10 percent a year. For the moment, he cannot afford to speculate. If he has less than $200,000 now, he'll have to alter his lifetime goal or accelerate his savings program. He certainly cannot afford to speculate. But what if he happens to have $220,000? That means he has $20,000 he does not need to achieve his goal of financial serenity. As painful as it might be, he can afford to lose that $20,000 without jeopardizing his future. Since he can afford to lose it, he can afford to speculate with it.

Everyone should be this methodical about figuring out what they can afford to risk, but not everyone is. Some people speculate because they find prudent investing a little dull. Speculation is certainly not dull. Others speculate just for the fun of it. Now, I happen to think that getting rich slowly with a careful investment program is a whole lot of fun. But there's no arguing with taste.

If you can truly afford to speculate, like our architect friend, you have my blessing to go wild. If you truly cannot but are looking for some thrills, I suggest you go to Coney Island.

Either way, here, for the record, is a lineup of speculative investments.

SPECULATIVE STOCKS

The definition of a speculative stock is elastic; one person's sound investment opportunity will look to someone else like a wild flyer. But, while all stocks entail a degree of risk, some stocks clearly entail more risk than others—and also offer potentially higher rewards.

One area of speculation on the stock market lies among "cyclical" stocks. These are the shares of companies in industries like automaking and construction that tend to do very well during periods of general economic prosperity and very poorly when times are hard. The reason why some industries are cyclical and some are not is fairly clear—if times are tough you can put off buying a new car until next year, but you cannot put off buying groceries until next year without getting awfully hungry. What is not clear is when an economic upturn is just around the corner. If the economy is depressed, and cyclical stocks are in the cellar, and you have a strong feeling that happy days are just about here again, then you can profit by buying cyclical stocks. But, since you have no way of *knowing* that the economy is about to improve, you may be buying them years too soon.

The major area of speculation on Wall Street is among "growth" stocks. All stocks, of course, are expected to grow; nobody would buy any stock that he expected to shrink. But it is also true that some stocks have more growth potential than others. The riskiest growth stocks are those that are *all* potential. These are often the shares of brand-new companies headed by people with bright new ideas. Such companies may have no track record of earnings performance to look back on, because they haven't gotten around yet to getting their exciting new product out into the market. But it's a dynamite concept, it really is, and as soon as all the financing is in place and the bugs are worked out of the time-travel circuit board, the company is really going to take off. Or so they say.

A few such companies really do take off. Most do not. While their fates are unravelling, their shares can generally be found trading for a few dollars (or less) on the "over-the-counter" market of stocks that are not listed on any stock exchange (but can, like listed stocks, be bought and sold through brokers).

Hot growth stocks tend to cluster, decade by decade, in particular industries. In the 1950s, for example, pharmaceuticals were hot. In the 1960s, the action shifted to high-technology companies and conglomerates. In the 1970s (for a while), oil stocks boomed. In the early 1980s, computer stocks were the rage. In every case, there was some sound reason underlying the popularity of the industry. As the world changes, there is *always* some new industry that seems to be pointing the way toward revolutionary changes in the way we live. (What do you hear about robotics?) The problem for investors is that, even if a new industry does change the world, not every company in that industry will prosper, or even survive. History records that pioneers often fall by the wayside. So even if you have decided, correctly, that microwave mailboxes are about to revolutionize American life, you may not be able to pick the right microwave mailbox company to buy into. If you do pick the right one, you might make a fortune. But you'd better be prepared for the consequences of guessing wrong.

Equally speculative are the shares of older companies that have fallen on hard times. There are always a few old companies whose stocks are selling at record lows. Often these are last year's hot growth issues, now battered down by investor disappointment or a generally sluggish market. Buying the shares of such companies for a few dollars apiece is like buying a "perpetual option" on their assets, future earnings, and prospects. These "perpetual options" may cost little more than actual stock options (described below). Unlike actual stock options, however, they have no expiration date and they do have some inherent value. Even if an ailing company goes bankrupt, shareholders may have some claim on its liquidated assets. If the company recovers, as some do, the speculation may pay off handsomely.

Another popular speculation in recent years has been to buy shares of companies considered to be possible objects of takeover attempts. (If a "corporate raider" does make a lucrative per-share offer for such a company, those who have bought its shares stand to make a quick profit.) It turned out, of course, that some of those "speculating" in takeover companies were not speculating at all; they had illegal inside information when takeover attempts were imminent. Thus they prudently reduced the risks of their speculation—except for the risk of going jail.

BUYING ON MARGIN

Some investors attempt to increase their profits by buying stocks on margin. They open a margin (or "general") account with a stockbroker, which allows them to buy securities with a 50 percent down payment. The broker provides a loan for the other 50 percent. The securities purchased are held in the margin account as collateral. Because the collateral is always on hand, minimizing the lender's risk, margin loan rates are relatively low, generally several points lower than banks charge for consumer loans (and miles below what they charge on credit card balances).[1]

Most people who buy stocks on margin do so to increase their leverage. If you buy $10,000 worth of stock for $10,000 and the value of the stock goes to $15,000, you have made 50 percent on your money (minus brokerage commissions). But if, by using a margin account, you buy $10,000 worth of stock for $5,000 and the value of the stock goes to $15,000, you have made 100 percent on your money (minus brokerage commissions and interest). Margin accounts thus make stock market investing work something like real estate investing, in which the use of leverage to increase rates of return is very common.

But leverage works both ways. If you buy $10,000 worth of stock for $5,000 and the value of the stock declines to $5,000, you have lost 100 percent of your investment. And you will, at the same time, be facing the discomfort of something known as a "margin call." Federal regulations require that your equity in a margin account (the value of the stock you own minus the amount you owe the broker) must always be at least 25 percent of the current market price of the stock. If you buy $10,000 worth of stock with $5,000 down and a $5,000 loan, your equity is 50 percent. But if the stock price drops to $6,667, your equity will be only 25 percent ($6,667 minus $5,000 equals $1,667,

---

[1]Using your securities as collateral, you can, in fact, borrow up to 50 percent of their market value from your broker for any purpose at the relatively low margin loan rate. You could save hundreds of dollars or more in interest payments by financing a new car, say, with a loan from your broker instead of other sources.

which is 25 percent of $6,667). At this point you must come up with some cash to repay part of your outstanding loan. If you don't have the cash, your broker will sell off some of your stock—at its depressed price—to raise the money. This can be an unhappy situation.

SELLING SHORT

Selling short is a technique for trading in stocks one does not own. Typically, an investor will buy a stock he does not own in the hope that its price will go up. A short seller does just the opposite: He sells a stock he does not own in the hope that its price will go down.

This is the way it works:

Joe Blow decides that the stock of International Zither Machines (IZM), currently selling for $100 a share, is overpriced and heading for a fall. I have no idea how or why Mr. Blow makes that decision. There is no way he can *know* that the price of the stock is about to fall (unless he is dealing with illegal inside information, in which case he can expect to receive a call from the SEC). No one can know that the price of *any* stock is about to fall (or rise). All short-term movements in the stock market are unpredictable. That's why no prudent investment program should involve trying to guess such short-term movements. But Mr. Blow is not involved in a prudent investment program here. He is speculating.

For reasons that satisfy him, Mr. Blow has decided that the price of IZM will shortly be dropping. So he goes out and sells 100 shares of the stock at the current price, $100. He doesn't own any IZM, however. He has just "sold short." So his broker arranges to borrow 100 shares of

IZM, on Mr. Blow's behalf, from someone who does own it. The borrowed shares are delivered to the buyer, and Mr. Blow pockets $10,000 from the sale. Now all he has to do is buy 100 shares of IZM and return them to the person who lent them to him. (Until he does, he is obligated to pay the lender, out of his own pocket, any dividends declared on the borrowed stock.)

If the price of IZM goes down, as Mr. Blow is hoping, then returning the borrowed stock will be a pleasure. If it goes down to $80, say, he'll buy 100 shares for $8,000, hand them over, and walk away from the deal with a $2,000 profit (before commissions and taxes, of course).

If the price of IZM goes up, however, there will be no joy at Mr. Blow's house. At $120 a share, it will cost him $12,000 to buy the shares he previously sold for $10,000. Net loss: $2,000 (plus the broker's commission on both the purchase and the previous short sale).

The life of a short seller is complicated by the fact that stocks may go up before they go down. Mr. Blow may be absolutely right about IZM. When he "shorts" it at $100, it may indeed be on its way down to $50, but he will have a very uncomfortable time of it if the stock drops to $50 only after first going *up* to $150.

This will create two problems for Mr. Blow. First, he may panic. As IZM climbs up and up, he may conclude that he was insane ever to think that it would go down and decide to cut his losses by buying it back at, say, $140, for a $4,000 loss.

Even if Mr. Blow does not despair, and remains steadfast in his conviction that IZM will fall, he may still be forced to take a loss. To guarantee that short sellers can afford to buy back the stock they have borrowed, federal regulations require that they maintain a cash balance in their brokerage account sufficient to buy back the stock at

whatever its current price is. As the price of IZM goes up
and up, Mr. Blow's broker will occasionally call to demand
that he deposit more cash in his account. And it is possible
that Mr. Blow may run out of cash before IZM hits its
peak. No matter that he is still confident that IZM will
fall. If he has already sold the house and rented out the
kids to keep up the balance required in his account, and
IZM *still* continues up, and he cannot come up with any
more cash, then the money already in his account will
automatically be used to buy back IZM—at a substantial
loss for him. If the stock plummets to 0 the next day, it
will be cold comfort to Mr. Blow that he was right after
all.

There is, by the way, a popular nonspeculative use of
short selling known as selling short "against the box."
Suppose you have bought 100 shares of IZM at $100, and
the following December the stock has gone to $150. You'd
like to take your $5,000 profit, but you don't want to take
it just yet. If you hold the stock one more month, your
profit will be recorded in the following tax year, which you
find advantageous. You fear, however, that before the
month is up IZM may drop in price. You can lock in your
profit *and* defer your taxes into the next year by short
selling 100 shares of IZM in December. Then, in January,
you sell your 100 shares and buy 100 shares to return
those you have borrowed (or simply repay the borrowed
shares with the ones you already own). Any loss you take
on your own shares will be exactly offset by your profit on
the short sale (and vice versa). So, no matter what happens to the price of the stock in the meantime, you make
your $5,000. And the profit is credited to the next tax
year.

STOCK OPTIONS

An option is the right to buy or sell a given number of shares of a specific stock at a specific price during a specific time period. An option to buy is a "call." An option to sell is a "put." This is how they work:

Joan Blow thinks the stock of IZM, selling at $100, is about to go up. She can do two things. She can buy 100 shares of IZM for $10,000, which is a lot of money. Or she can buy a "call," giving her the option of buying 100 shares of IZM at, say, $105 anytime within the next six months. The call might cost her $500. (The exact price of a call will vary according to how close the option price is to the current stock price, how "volatile" the stock is—that is, how much it tends to bounce up and down in price, how long the option has to run, and what the general feeling is about the prospects for the stock.)

Now assume Ms. Blow was correct. IZM goes to $120 before the six months are up. If she had purchased the stock for $10,000, she could now sell it for $12,000, or a 20 percent profit (minus brokerage commissions). If she had purchased the $500 option instead, however, she could now exercise the option, buy the stock for $10,500 and immediately sell it for $12,000. This would give her a net profit of $1,000, or 200 percent on her original investment (minus, of course, brokerage commissions). Thus, stock options offer speculators far greater "leverage" than they can get by purchasing the underlying stocks instead.

But what if Ms. Blow was wrong about IZM, and the stock dropped to $80 and stayed there? If she had purchased 100 shares for $10,000, she would be looking at a $2,000 loss. If she had purchased the $500 option, however, she would only be out that $500. She would let the option expire without exercising it, and that would be that. Option buyers can never lose more than the cost of the option, no matter how low the price of the underlying stock falls.

All of this makes options a terrific way to make money, as long as you're pretty good at predicting which way particular stocks are going to move in the near future. And we all know how easy that is, right?

Option buyers also face a problem common to all low-cost investments. Commissions are high relative to the amount invested. (You could call this "commission leverage.") With investments like these, you have to win substantially more than you lose just to break even.

"Put" options work just the opposite of calls. You can buy one giving you the right to sell IZM at some price lower than its current price if you expect the stock to go down. If the stock falls below the price you have selected, you can make a substantial profit. If it goes up instead, you will lose your money.

Some of those who have done the best with options in recent years have *sold* call options instead of buying them. If you own 100 shares of IZM at $100, you might sell a $105 call option for $500. If the stock advances above $105 before the option expires, you will have to sell it at less than market value (but still at a profit). If it does not go above $105, you simply pocket the $500 from the option. Added to the dividends paid by your stock, the money you get from selling these "covered" options amounts to a very nice rate of return on your investment.

"Warrants," by the way, are similar to call options. They are securities issued by a corporation giving the holder the right to buy a specified number of shares of the company's stock at a specified price. Warrants are often given away by corporations as "sweeteners" with bonds of less than the highest rating. Thereafter, they are bought and sold by investors just as options are.

COMMODITY FUTURES

A commodities future contract is a commitment to buy or sell a specified commodity at a specified future time at a price agreed upon today. A typical contract might call for the delivery of thirty thousand pounds of live hogs four months from tomorrow at a price of 47.17 cents a pound. A speculator who thinks the price of hogs will rise in the next four months will buy such a contract. If hogs go up to 50 cents a pound, he will make a profit. A speculator who thinks the price of hogs will go down will sell such a contract. This is similar to the short sale of a stock; the speculator is selling hogs he does not own, hoping to buy them at a lower price before delivery is due.

Neither the buyer nor the seller, in most cases, will ever come anywhere near an actual live hog. Before the contract's specified delivery date, they will "close out" their positions by buying or selling a contract that offsets the one they previously sold or bought and taking their profit or loss. Nobody wants to see a truck pull into their driveway one morning and hear the driver shout, "Hey, lady, where do you want your pigs?"

Speculators in commodity futures (which are also available for cattle, wheat, corn, coffee, pork bellies, orange juice, lumber, and other items) can win or lose large amounts of money in a very short time. Commodity prices are very changeable, and commodity futures are highly leveraged. That is, one can buy or sell a futures contract by putting down a relatively small cash deposit; a few cents change in the price of the commodity can then double your money—or wipe you out.

It is, in fact, well documented that the vast majority of all individual speculators in commodity futures lose money. You really ought to stay away from the commodities markets unless you happen to be in the business of buying pigs, corn, oats, orange juice, or other commodities for actual use. If you are the Kellogg Company, you do belong in the commodities market, because of the practice known as "hedging." You—the Kellogg Company—are looking forward to selling cornflakes now and indefinitely into the future. You know that the price of corn fluctuates, but you don't want the price of cornflakes to fluctuate, because that makes cornflake buyers nervous. You have your pricing (and profit) scheme all worked out for the next year, based on the price of corn today, which might be $1.80 a bushel. You don't want to have to raise and lower the price of cornflakes every month as the price of corn goes up and down. So you buy futures contracts for the delivery of corn all through the year at $1.80 a bushel (plus some premium for what it will cost somebody, or would cost you, to buy the corn now and store it until it is needed). You might buy these contracts from farmers who are themselves hedging. They want to know right now what price they will get in six months for the corn they planted yesterday. Or you might buy these contracts from speculators who are betting that the price of corn will go down before they have to make delivery. But you don't care anymore what happens to the price of corn. You have protected your position by taking advantage of the commodities futures market.

But *you*, dear reader, are probably not the Kellogg Company. You have no position to protect in the futures market, only a great deal to lose.

In addition to commodities that grow in the ground and walk about in barnyards, futures contracts are also available in gold, silver, and other metals. Some people buy gold futures as a way of betting that inflation will soon be rising (gold always goes up with inflation), since buying gold futures requires less cash and complications than buying actual gold.

Futures contracts are also available on U.S. Treasury securities and other financial instruments. These provide a way of betting that interest rates will be rising or falling.

Finally, futures contracts are available on foreign currencies, providing a way of betting on the rise or fall of the French franc, for example. These are very useful to people who expect to be buying or selling something to France in the next few months and want to protect their profit margin by hedging against a fluctuation in the exchange rates. Unless you happen to be importing boatloads of Camembert and berets, however, you probably have no more business speculating in foreign currency futures than you do in live hogs.

STOCK INDEX OPTIONS

Stock index options have been around only a few years, but they have generated a great deal of excitement among people looking for a way to speculate on the general direction of the stock market. Unlike stock options, which involve the right to buy or sell shares of an actual stock, stock index options grant the right to buy or sell an abstraction. There is no such thing as a "stock index" that you can hold in your hand as you can a pork belly or a share of General Motors. A stock index is just a number, derived from averaging the prices of selected actual stocks. The most popular stock index option (several are traded on various exchanges) is based on one hundred blue-chip stocks and called the Standard & Poor 100.

If the S & P 100 stands at 280 (as it did in mid-1987), and you think that stock prices in general are about to go up, you might buy an option to buy the index at 285. If the index advances (which it will if the market in general advances), you will make money. If it declines, you will lose. As with all options, you benefit from leverage (your actual cash investment is small compared to the amount of money you can make), and your loss is limited to the price you have paid for the option.

In addition to stock index options, you may also speculate nowadays in stock index futures, which work just like commodity futures, except that there is no "there" there. Even if you hold the futures contract until the delivery date, nothing is delivered—except a check or a bill.

And, if all that isn't enough, the mind of man has now invented options on stock index futures. These give you the right to buy or sell at a specified price during a specified period a contract to deliver or take delivery of a stock index at a specified time at a specified price, except that nothing really would be delivered, because there is no such animal as a stock index.

If you can figure that one out, drop me a line.

SWINDLES

Some of the greatest speculations of all are simply lies. Often these lies are told over the telephone by faceless salespeople working in out-of-state "boiler rooms." They call prospect after prospect and tell a story about a great opportunity in oil leases on government land, or "strategic" metals, or fancy maneuvers in the international currency market, or some other complicated and almost plausible investment that sounds a little like something you have just been reading about in the newspapers or in *Forbes*. The salesmen on the telephone offer convincing reasons why their deals are generating fabulous payoffs, and why you have to invest right now, today, with no delay, or you will miss this unbelievable, one-of-a-kind investment opportunity of a lifetime.

Don't believe it. Don't buy. Hang up. Recognize that the voice inside you urging "Go for it!" is the voice of greed, not the voice of reason. Remember, if it sounds too good to be true, it is. There is no Santa Claus, and, if there were, he wouldn't be calling you on a WATS line from Waycross, Georgia, with a fantastic story about the profit potential of palladium.

CHAPTER 10

MANAGING YOUR PORTFOLIO

GETTING RICHER

I know a man who moves a lot. This is a great inconvenience, but his career requires it. And it does offer him one useful opportunity. Every time he moves, all of his belongings end up piled in the middle of his new living room. (And reorganizing his desk brings him face to face with records of financial assets not kept around the house.) Gazing at the accumulation of his worldly goods, he can make a quick estimation: Is the pile bigger than it was the last time he moved? Is he moving, asset-wise, in the right direction?

Accumulating capital, building your net worth, approaching your goal of financial serenity, is a task of many years. You cannot seek to do it with one quick killing. It will require planning, discipline, and time. Yet, as particular investments come and go, and milestones in your life roll by, there will inevitably be times when you lose sight of the big picture. The main focus of that picture should be your progress. *Are* you getting richer?

You *should* be, if you have followed the general principles we have already discussed and put your money into some of the specific investment vehicles we have described. But there is more to a successful investment program than we have covered so far. Investments do not take care of themselves, even in the hands of an able broker. You must prune them and tend them and evaluate them regularly. You must, in short, *manage* them. There follow, therefore, some rules and suggestions for the care and feeding of a lifetime investment program.

DIVERSIFICATION BY TYPE

First of all, it should have a varied diet. Obviously, you would be foolish to put all your money into the stock, or bonds, of one company. That would leave you vulnerable to being wiped out if that single company encountered hard times. What if it's discovered that widgets cause cancer? Or the federal government suddenly imposes a fifty-five-mile-per-hour speed limit on widgets? Or the Japanese find a way to make widgets out of seawater? Or an earthquake opens up behind the headquarters of Worldwide Widget, and the company falls in? No good. You've got to be diversified, to spread out your risk.

It is not quite so obvious, but it would also be foolish to concentrate your money in a single *type* of asset. If your portfolio consists entirely of fixed-income investments— bonds, certificates of deposit, and other types of "lending" investments that pay predetermined interest rates—you are vulnerable to inflation. Should soaring inflation ever return and its rate exceed your locked-in rates of return, you would have to watch helplessly as your net worth declined. If you own only common stocks, on the other hand, you are protected from the worst effects of inflation, but you are vulnerable to the effects of a major recession.

A well-balanced portfolio should include both fixed-income investments and common stocks. And neither component of your program should consist of a single security. You should own different stocks (or a stock mutual fund) and several different bonds (or a bond mutual fund or unit investment trust). Your portfolio might also include some "hands-off" real estate investments like limited partnerships and real estate investment trusts, and you might choose to own as well some "hard assets" such as gold or silver.

To visualize where you stand already, it might be useful to draw a bar graph representing your assets. Assign a different color to each type of asset (fixed-income, common stocks, real estate, gold, and collectibles). You might be surprised to see a single color dominating the chart. You may never before have realized how heavily weighted your portfolio is toward real estate if your main asset is your house, or how it tilts toward fixed-income investments if most of your money is in bank accounts, money market funds, and traditional whole-life insurance policies (all of which *are* fixed-income investments). If a single color dominates your bar graph, you must work toward making it a rainbow.

DIVERSIFICATION OVER TIME

Frequently overlooked but just as important as diversification by type of investment is diversification by *time*. It is a principle that applies to all investments but is especially relevant to stocks.

Suppose you have reached, as you inevitably should, a decision to invest a portion of your net worth in stocks. You and your broker have selected a short list of stocks for your portfolio. Wisely, you are not planning on putting all your money into a single company. You've chosen half a dozen stocks, all in different industries. You've picked companies that you have good reason to believe are well positioned to create real wealth over the long term. They are competently managed, and they (and their industries) are not the Fad of the Month (which could mean that they were ludicrously overpriced). You're ready to buy. You show up at your broker's office with check in hand. Take my money, you say. It's burning a hole in my money market fund. Call up Wall Street and get me in.

Slow down.

Think for a minute. You know how the market is. It goes up *and* down. Up a bit, then down a bit, then down some more. Then up, then down. Then down. Then up. Odds are, in the long run it is going up to stay. It always has. Odds are, in the long run the stocks you have selected will go up too. Most do. But the long road up will be obscured by countless detours up and down. It always is.

At any given moment, it is impossible to know whether the market is high or low. We can only guess where it stands in the corkscrew minicycles through which it endlessly gyrates. Some of the reasons for the daily ups and downs seem apparent. A bill to cut taxes is approved by a Senate committee. Interest rates move down. The President recovers from his laryngitis. Other market moves are totally inexplicable. Some people say they can be predicted by sunspot activity. Really. Others say they are linked to who won the last Super Bowl.

But all we know for sure is this. When you hear the news announcer lead off his twenty-second business report by saying, "Investors nervous about the Middle East brought the market down today," or "The market rose as Wall Street anticipated a drop in widget prices"—there's no way he can *know* those things to be true. If he, or anyone else, knew why the market moved the way it did on any particular day, they would be multibillionaires. And they're not.

So, as the market unpredictably bounces up and down, there you stand on the sidelines, check in hand, ready to dive in. The prudent thing to do—since you cannot know if the market is bouncing up or bouncing down—is not to jump in all at once. If you're planning on investing $25,000 in eight stocks (about $3,000 per stock), buy three of the stocks today and put the remaining $16,000 back in your money market fund. A couple of months from now, take out another $9,000 and buy three more stocks. Wait another couple of months, and then buy the rest.

And don't be upset if the market moves in the meantime. It's going to, and you won't die of it. If the market moves up before you have completed your purchases, then you'll pay more for some of your stocks than you would have if you had bought them all at once. But so what? The stocks you bought first have gone up. You're already ahead. Congratulations.

If the market goes down, don't be alarmed. You've picked your stocks for good reasons, and even a major market drop does not necessarily alter the fundamental value of the companies. If their stock prices have fallen, so much the better. When you buy them, you're getting a bargain.

The real benefit of this diversification over time is that you buy into the market at something approaching an average price and avoid the risk of making your entire investment at what turns out to be a temporary peak. (Logic might seem to call for buying your stocks one at a time, instead of in groups of two or three, but, emotionally, that is a risky way to proceed. If you begin your program by buying a single stock, and that stock promptly falls in price, you may be too discouraged to continue. If you buy three stocks to begin, at least one should go up, or, if there's a general market decline, one will go down less than the others—a moral victory.)

This approach, carried to an extreme, is called "dollar-cost averaging," and is a very sensible way to invest. It calls for investing the same amount of money at regular intervals in the same stocks. Say, for example, that you have $1,200 a year to invest. You decide to dollar-cost average, so you will put $100 on the first of every month into General Bones, which you are convinced has excellent long-term prospects. (You should not be investing in a single stock, of course, but we'll concentrate on General Bones for the sake of this example.) On January 1, the stock is selling for $10, so you get 10 shares for your $100. By February 1, the stock has collapsed to $5, but you do not panic—this is crucial—and again you invest $100. This time it buys you 20 shares. In mid-February the bone market explodes and by March 1 your stock is at $15. For your $100 you get 6.7 shares. By April 1 the bone hysteria is over and the stock is back at $10, right where it began. You buy 10 more shares.

How do you stand? The stock sank five points below its starting point, then rose five points above its starting point, then went back to where it began. You're even, right?

Wrong. You are ahead. Figure it out. Your total investment was $400. You have purchased 46.7 shares. You can sell them today (with the stock back at $10) for $467. Good going.

What happened here is testimony both to your original strategy and to your strength of will. When General Bones sank to $5, you did not panic and bail out. You kept buying, and, because the price was down, you got more shares for your $100. (Conversely, when the price was up, you got fewer shares for your $100.) Dollar-cost-averaging is a reliable strategy that gives you significant protection from the ups and downs of the market. In fact, those movements can make you money. As long as the company doesn't go broke, you will eventually come out ahead.

THE VIRTUES OF PATIENCE

Of course, you will not be buying General Bones or anything else if you have not yet begun to convert some of your income dollars to capital dollars. The necessity not to spend all that you earn underlies everything else in this book, and it has either sunk in by now or you are wasting your time by continuing to read.

Once you *have* accumulated the capital to buy some stocks and you have purchased a small portfolio, diversified by company, industry, and time, what then? How do you know when to buy more and, more to the point, when to sell?

The ideal strategy, of course, would be to buy low and sell high. Buy stocks only at or near their all-time lows and proceed to sell them at or near their all-time highs. This is a lovely strategy, but you would have to be God to practice it. No mere mortal can know when these highs and lows are occurring. Tomorrow may see a lower low or a higher high. Until you learn to see into the future, you had better have a different plan.

Our basic rule is to sit. On Wall Street, it is frequently a fact that "more money is made sitting than thinking." Certainly many of the largest American fortunes have been made by acquiring assets and holding them. The only way I myself have ever made money in the stock market is by buying a good stock and holding on to it. This strategy can also work for you.

It will probably test your patience, however. And it may test other aspects of your personality as well. Many of you who have the capability and desire to get rich slowly are undoubtedly driven by the "Puritan ethic." You cannot believe that any worthwhile activity you engage in requires less than 110 percent of your time and energy. This may be true of many human activities, but it can be counterproductive in investing.

Successful investing requires that you identify good value in companies that are effective in creating wealth, that you then associate yourself, through your capital, with those companies, and that you, finally, sit and hold their stocks over the years while your judgment is vindicated. Don't assume that by doing nothing you're "doing nothing"; the game really can be that easy.

The Puritan ethic *will* play a role in your success, but indirectly. The people running the companies you have selected should be consumed by it—but you should not. While they work day and night to make your companies successful, you must resist the urge to think excessively about the stocks, to worry about them, to trade them, to sell them when the market is high, to buy them back when the market is low. If you start playing those games you will inevitably lose. You will end up selling too soon and buying too late. You will be outsmarted at least 50 percent of the time by the people from whom you are buying and selling (unless you have the unbelievable good luck to encounter repeatedly stock traders who are in the process of squandering inherited fortunes). If you win half the time you will still lose because of brokerage commissions and other transaction costs.

So relax. Take it easy. Buy, and sit.

The hardest part of this will be disciplining yourself to ignore the "noise" of up-and-down market movements. The market is always going up and down, but most of those movements have nothing to do with the value of the stocks you have selected. It will not be easy for you to remember this. When your stocks go down you will be convinced you have made terrible misjudgments in buying them. (Occasionally this will be true; usually it will not.) When your stocks go up you may decide you are a stock market genius and be emboldened to start "playing the market," which, I assure you, will be a costly mistake. The market goes up and the market goes down. *Do not take it personally*.

KEEP WINNERS, SELL LOSERS

So our basic rule is buy and hold. But (and you've been expecting this "but," haven't you?) that does not mean that you should be pigheaded. Sometimes you will make a mistake. And sometimes there will occur fundamental changes in the economy or the marketplace or the management of one of your companies to which you should react. I once knew a man who had a lot of gilt-edged ferry bonds, and then somebody built a bridge.

In managing your portfolio, your tactic should be to keep the winners and weed out the losers, always keeping in mind that not every stock that goes down *is* a loser. All stock prices dip from time to time, usually in tandem with the rest of the market. This "noise" is a different phenomenon than the slide of a company that has developed a serious problem.

The tactic of keeping winners and selling losers, while it may seem obvious, is in fact just the opposite of what most people do. When a stock goes up, they sell it, take their profit, tell everybody how smart they are, and look for something else to buy. When a stock goes down, they hold on for dear life, waiting for it to rise back to its former level, although there is no good reason why it should. Inevitably, by selling their winners and holding their losers, such people end up in the unhappy position of owning a portfolio of stocks all of which are losers.

These loser-holders often operate on the theory that "it's not a loss until I take it." Or they hold their positions out of simple lethargy, believing that it's wisest to leave poor enough alone. Or they feel loyal to a stock, as if it were a human being. "IBM has been good to me," they say, looking back to past successes. But take my word for it, IBM doesn't even *know* you. Do not fall in love with a stock. It will not return the favor. When you have made a mistake, and it is clear that you own a turkey, sell it. There is no point in postponing the day of reckoning. A loss *is* a loss, even before you sell it. So sell it now, take your tax loss, and put the money into something better.

There are also times when you should sell winners, despite the general rule to hold them. Sometimes you are fortunate enough to pick an unpopular, undervalued stock that a year or two later becomes the fad of the moment and gets driven up to an inflated price that has little to do with the company's underlying value. Sell. Sometimes you own a stock that becomes the object of a bidding war in a takeover attempt. Sell. In general, sell if circumstances make a stock overpriced. Do not sell if the stock is only rising in price to or near its actual value (which attracted you to the stock in the first place). The best may be yet to come.

MEASURING PERFORMANCE

As time goes by, you will want to monitor the performance of the stocks you own (and thus, indirectly, the performance of the broker who recommended them). To be meaningful, these evaluations must be more complicated than simply noting which stocks are up and which are down.

Stock performance must be measured in comparison with market trends. If your stocks are down 5 percent while the market as a whole is down 15 percent, then they (and your broker) are performing heroically. If your stocks are up 10 percent while the market is up 20 percent, wipe that grin off your face. You are not doing as well as you should be.

An additional complication in evaluating the performance of a stock is the difficulty of separating "real" price movement from the distracting background of market "noise." Here is a graph of the price movement of a stock (movement that will typically coincide more or less with the movement of the market as a whole):

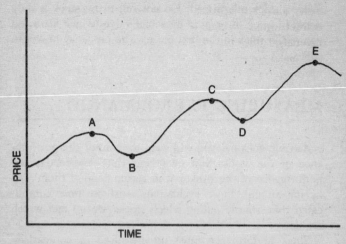

If you bought the stock at point A and evaluate its performance at point B, you will be very unhappy. (You will probably blame your broker for your unhappiness, and fire him or her.) If you bought at point B and evaluate at point C, you will be ecstatic. (You will probably credit yourself entirely for your success and congratulate your broker only for being wise enough to select you as a client.) In both cases, your conclusions will be wrong.

The best measure of the stock's performance is to compare peak to peak (point A to point C to point E) or trough to trough (point B to point D). Measured that way, this stock is doing nicely. The only way to take this measurement, however, is from a long perspective. You never know at any given moment whether you are at a peak or a trough or somewhere in between. Only months or years later can you look back and see the picture clearly. This is one more reason to hold the stocks you buy, barring fundamental changes in their underlying value. Historically, most stocks have moved up from market cycle to market cycle. If you choose your stocks carefully and diversify sufficiently to compensate for the mistakes you will make anyway, then your portfolio, on average, should move up too.

MOVING TOWARD YOUR GOAL

The most important evaluations you will make as the years go by will be those that measure your progress, or lack thereof, toward your ultimate goal.

As I've said before, you must define a goal for yourself—to have $500,000 by age sixty-two, to have $800,000 by age sixty-eight, to have $1.98 by next Tuesday, *something*. Without a definite goal, you will have no idea if you are reaching it.

Once your goal is established, you can calculate what combination of savings and investment growth you must achieve to reach it. Buy a pad of graph paper (or a graphics/spreadsheet program for your personal computer). Spend some time plotting where various rates of savings and compound interest will lead you from your present situation. Plot where you must be every six months for the next ten years to meet your goal. You will see exactly how easy and how hard it is.

Your task will be hopeless if your goals are unreasonable. Remember, you cannot count on finding $10 stocks that will go to $15 in six months, or one year, or two. Aiming for too high a rate of return will lead you into taking speculative risks that will almost certainly wreck your entire program. To repeat basic principles: Seek a reasonable rate of return. Start investing early. Let years of compound interest work for you.

Then, once or twice a year, calculate your net worth. See if you are meeting the targets on your graph. See how much of your income has been converted to capital, and how fast your capital is growing. If you are falling behind, you must rethink your investments, or increase your savings, or both.

It is not unreasonable for you to plan on becoming a millionaire. As of 1987, there were 1,300,000 millionaires in the United States. There is always room for one more. Sixty-four dollars a week invested at 10 percent interest starting at age thirty will grow to a million dollars by age sixty-five.

Achieving that goal, or a comparable one, will truly bring you to a state of financial serenity. Monitoring your progress, along the way, seeing your investments succeed and your assets pile up, watching your net worth grow from year to year, will spread that serenity throughout your entire life.

Is the effort worth it? My mother always told me, "Bob, it's just as easy to fall in love with a rich girl as a poor one." Let me paraphrase that now: "It's almost as easy to go through life getting rich as staying poor. And it feels a whole lot better."

CHAPTER 11

ECONOMIC FACTS OF LIFE

THE INDIVIDUAL AND THE ECONOMY

Judging from the headlines, the situation is hopeless. The dollar is up—American workers are losing their jobs because of cheap imports. The dollar is down—people are losing confidence in the American economy. Inflation is up—your real income is declining. Inflation is down—chaos in the real estate market. Interest rates are up—businesses can't afford to expand. Interest rates are down—your savings aren't growing very fast. The federal deficit is up—every new American baby is born $9,000 in debt.

What's a person to do?

News reports about the economy seem to stress the negative consequences of every development, and they often portray the individual as a helpless victim buffeted by ceaselessly harmful economic storms. So it's not surprising that many people glance at the financial pages of their newspapers with resignation, sighing at the latest news they barely understand. All that's made clear to them is that whatever the news is—interest rates up or interest rates down—it almost certainly isn't going to do them any good.

In fact, the news is *not* as bad as it seems. How could it be? The economy does roll on in complex and unpredictable ways, as it always has and always will, but most of the moves in its erratic course produce both losers *and* winners.

The only sure thing about the economy is that it will change, and that those caught on the wrong side of the change will be losers—at least until the next change in the opposite direction. Of course, *some* changes are fundamental. It does not appear that the American steel industry, for example, is about to recover its former prosperity. For the indefinite future, it will not be a good idea for high school students to count on careers in the mills. The decline of American steel is part of a global realignment of economic activity. Between 1979 and 1984, 6 percent of American manufacturing jobs disappeared. They were more than replaced, however, by jobs in service industries and new technologies, many of which did not even exist when the steel mills were last going strong. The world changes, and it is a sign of maturity, both personal and national, to accept major changes and to adapt to them.

Much of the financial news, however, deals with changes that are short-term—the dollar up, the dollar down, recession today, recovery tomorrow—and you don't have to sell your house in Pittsburgh because of them. If you keep your head and try to understand what is happening—and what is not—you can weather these periodic economic crises, and maybe even profit from some of them.

THE SPECTER OF INFLATION

Take inflation.

Everybody knows that during the late 1970s and early 1980s America endured an unprecedented period of high inflation. Well, maybe not entirely unprecedented. What Americans went through in those years certainly did not compare with the German hyperinflation of the early 1920s, when prices rose one trillion percent in twenty-two months, until it cost 100,000,000,000 marks to mail a letter. Nor did our 1970s experience compare with the inflation Americans suffered following the Revolutionary War, when the purchasing power of the Continental dollar dropped to one thousandth of its original value. Nor did the American 1970s compare to the inflation still raging today in Argentina, Israel, and many other countries.

Nevertheless, what happened to most of us in the 1970s came as a shock, largely because we had had no recent experience with inflation. During most of the 1950s and early 1960s, the annual inflation rate was less than 2 percent, and sometimes less than 1 percent. People seriously suggested that inflation might be gone forever.

But it returned, as it always does, and at first, Americans didn't mind it very much. People's salaries were going up, the value of their homes was going up, and business profits were going up. It made people feel prosperous to have more money to spend, even if, because of rising prices, they had to spend it all.

Once people caught on to what was happening, however, a vicious circle started to turn. It's one thing to get an unexpected 10 percent raise and then notice, gee whiz, that prices just happen to have gone up 10 percent too. It's another thing when you start to *expect* prices to go up

10 percent a year. Then, when you're negotiating for your next raise, you're going to demand (quite reasonably) that your salary go up not just 10 percent, because that would only keep you even, but, say, 15 percent. If your employer gives you and your coworkers 15 percent raises, then, even if he hadn't previously planned on it, the prices of the products he manufactures are definitely going to be going up at least 10 percent next year.

In an inflationary cycle, this pattern begins to spread through the economy. Labor contracts begin to contain cost-of-living escalators, guaranteeing that wages will go up when prices do. And prices do, so wages go up, which raises manufacturing costs, which causes prices to go up, which causes wages to go up. And so on.

This pattern of inflation as a self-fulfilling prophecy took hold in the United States in the late 1970s. What had cost $1 to buy in 1970 cost $2.47 in 1980. But this was not bad news for everybody. People who had bought $30,000 homes in 1965 with 6 percent mortgages found that their houses were now worth $100,000 and that the monthly mortgage payments they had worried so much about being able to afford back in 1965 now looked like busfare.

The banks and savings and loan associations collecting those piddling little mortgage payments were not so pleased, however. Neither were people on pensions and other fixed incomes that were not "indexed" to go up when inflation did. Imagine a couple who had retired about 1959. At the time, they congratulated themselves for having shrewdly managed their financial affairs so that they were guaranteed a retirement income of $800 a month, *for life*. This looked pretty good in 1959. By 1979, they were desperate. These people had made their financial arrangements during a prolonged period of low inflation. They had made the mistake of assuming that what had been would continue to be. In economic affairs, that's just not so. Inflation, like the tide, always returns.

It was little solace to our newly impoverished couple and people like them, but, during the 1970s, a new generation of investors made the identical, but opposite, mistake. Because they were living during a prolonged period of inflation, they assumed that *that* would continue. So they bet on it, and they lost.

INTEREST RATES, REAL PROPERTY, AND INFLATION

Whether individuals win or lose during an inflationary period has a great deal to do with interest rates. An interest rate is a way of measuring the rate of return on an investment. You put your money in a savings account, and the bank will pay you 5.5 percent a year for the use of your money. That's all well and good—unless the rate of inflation is more than 5.5 percent. If it is, then the value of your money (that is, the amount of goods you can buy with it) will actually be decreasing while it is sitting in your savings account earning interest.

While the interest rates on simple savings accounts are fixed, the rates on more sophisticated investments are in a constant state of flux. The United States Treasury, for example, sells three-month Treasury bills every Monday at Federal Reserve Banks. Those who buy these "bills" are making short-term loans to the United States government; at the end of three months they will be repaid (unless the United States government collapses in the meantime).

How does the government set the interest rate on these loans? It doesn't. The bills are sold in an auction system.

Investors bid on them, and the bills go to those who are willing to accept the lowest rate of return on that particular Monday. What that rate is depends on several factors, one of the most important of which is what is happening—and what investors expect to happen—to the rate of inflation. If inflation is currently running at 10 percent, nobody is going to bid to buy a Treasury bill paying 8 percent. If inflation is running at 5 percent, then 8 percent is just about right.

Seasoned investors do not focus on the "nominal" interest rate of an investment; they keep their eyes on its "real" interest rate. The real rate is the difference between the nominal (or stated) interest rate of an investment and the current rate of inflation. If your money is in a bank account paying 5.5 percent interest and the inflation rate is 5.5 percent, then your nominal interest rate is 5.5 percent, but your real interest rate is zero. Five-and-a-half minus five-and-a-half equals zero. The purchasing power of your money is not increasing at all.

Historically, investors have expected a real rate of return of about 3 or 4 percent on safe investments. Short-term Treasury bills are about the safest investment around, so they generally end up selling for 3 to 4 percent above the current inflation rate.

During the inflationary 1970s, inexperienced investors, who didn't know a thing about three-month Treasury bills, gradually caught on that their money wasn't doing them very much good in savings accounts. In 1979, for example, while banks were paying 5.5 percent on savings, the cost of living went up 13 percent. So the real interest rate on a savings account that year was negative, –7.5 percent. At that rate, thanks to the wonders of compound interest, any money you had in a savings account would rapidly shrink toward nothing.

Fortunately for the average investor, changes in the banking laws and innovations in financial services during the 1970s opened up new, higher-interest methods of saving. Money market funds and certificates of deposit, paying substantially higher rates of interest than savings accounts, were made available to people of moderate means, and many took advantage of them. For the first time, Mr. and Mrs. North America could get access to the same financial instruments as large institutions.

Some individuals looked for even more profitable ways of staying ahead of inflation. They began to buy *things*. It was the price of things, after all, that was going up year after year, while the value of money was decreasing. So people began to buy all kinds of things—gold, rare stamps, Oriental rugs, antique cars, antique Barbie dolls, you name it. The value of precious metals and collectibles soared.

The most popular thing of all during the heart of the inflation was real estate. Land and housing prices seemed to be going up without end. In some areas, like Manhattan and Los Angeles, the escalation in real estate prices was truly astronomical. It seemed that you could not possibly lose buying real estate in those markets. Buy something today, sell it next year, and make a pile of money. I know of one man in Los Angeles who, at the peak of the real estate boom, was driving to the airport to pick up his wife. By the side of the freeway, he saw a new condominium complex just beginning construction. A sign in front of it said that units were available for sale. He pulled off the freeway and bought five.

Real estate investments like this were especially profitable because of leverage. If you buy a $100,000 condominium for $100,000 cash and sell it a year later for $120,000 you have made 20 percent on your money. Not bad. But what if you buy a $100,000 condominium for $20,000 down and take out a mortgage to pay for the rest? If you sell the unit a year later for $120,000, you have made $20,000 on an actual cash investment of only $20,000. So you have made 100 percent of your money (less carrying charges). This is leverage in action. It made a lot of money for a lot of people.

In fact, the people who made out best during the inflationary period were those who owned a lot of property, owed a lot of money, and had very little cash. Consider two families:

The Browns own a house worth $100,000. They are very proud of the fact that they have paid off most of their mortgage; they owe the bank only $20,000. They have also been scrupulous about putting aside money for a rainy day; their savings total $50,000. Their net worth is thus $100,000 minus $20,000 plus $50,000, for a total of $130,000.

Their neighbors are the Greens. The Greens too own a house worth $100,000, but they have taken a second mortage on it to make a down payment on a vacation home. The value of that house is also $100,000. Between two first mortgages and one second mortgage, the Greens are $160,000 in debt. They have $10 in the bank. Their net worth is thus $100,000 plus $100,000 minus $160,000 plus $10, for a total of $40,010.

Then inflation strikes. Prices double. Interest rates paid on cash investments barely keep even with inflation, for a real interest rate of 0 percent. Where do our families stand?

The Browns' house is now worth $200,000. They still owe $20,000 to the bank and they still have $50,000 in cash investments. So their new net worth is $230,000. However, since prices have doubled, money is worth only half what it used to be. Adjusted for inflation, their new net worth is only $115,000. Because of the decline in the purchasing power of the dollar, they have effectively lost money during the inflationary period.

And the Greens? Their houses are now worth $200,000 each. They still owe the bank $160,000 and they still have $10 in a savings account. Their net worth is now $240,010. Adjusted for inflation, that is equivalent to $120,005 "original-year" dollars. Inflation has been very kind to the Greens.

This example is over simplified, of course. It does not take into account the interest that the Greens would have had to pay on their loans during the years it took for the value of their properties to double. How this affected their profits would have been determined by when the loans were made. If they were made before the oncoming inflation was apparent, when mortgage interest rates were still fixed at less than 8 percent (which they were as late as 1973), then the Greens would have done even better than the above figures indicate, because the bank would have been receiving a negative real interest rate on its loans during the height of the inflation.

Not every borrower got into the game that early, however. In fact, a lot of people got into the game at exactly the wrong time. They borrowed money to buy property *after* interest rates had risen to take inflation into account. But they shrugged that off. So what if the interest rate on their loans was high? The real estate inflation rate was even higher. They could always sell out in a couple of years and make enough profit on their properties to cover the high cost of the loan. Right?

These late-arriving borrowers failed to take into account the one sure thing about the economy—that it will change. After a decade of high inflation, and several fruitless attempts to slow it down, the Reagan administration and the Federal Reserve Board took measures that finally succeeded. They were harsh—the cure for inflation required a deep recession and high unemployment—but they worked. (The Reaganites also got a lucky break; oil prices broke.) By 1982, the inflation rate had dipped to less than 4 percent.

When the switch in the trend came, it took interest rates a while to adjust. It always does, for investors tend to assume that what has been happening in the economy for the last few years will continue to happen. Therefore, when inflation first took off in the 1970s, interest rates had lagged behind. The real interest rate on Treasury securities, usually 3 to 4 percent, was actually negative for periods immediately following the sharpest inflation peaks of the decade. During those months, the Treasury (and other borrowers) got a very good deal. Lenders were burned.

When inflation dipped in the early 1980s, the tables turned. Investors didn't believe they could trust the new low-inflation trend to continue, so interest rates stayed high. The real interest rate on Treasury securities was, for a while, 8 percent. Lenders did very well for themselves.

But borrowers were in plenty of trouble.

By the end of 1984, home mortgage foreclosures had reached their highest point in more than a decade. Tens of thousands of families found they couldn't afford their high-interest mortgage payments. A few years before, they could have resolved the situation by selling their houses at a profit, paying off their mortgages, and buying smaller houses. But real estate values had levelled off. Many people could not sell their houses at a profit. So they lost them. "Had home inflation not halted," said an official of the Federal Housing Administration, "it might have bailed out most of those who got in trouble."

Real estate speculators across the country—like the man

who bought five condominiums on his way to the airport—faced the same trouble, for leverage works both ways. Just as it enables investors to make 100 percent on their money in a single year when property values are racing up, so does it enable them to lose 100 percent of their money in a single year when property values come down. During the great boom of the 1970s, speculators had their cake—and they ate it.

THE FEDERAL DEFICIT

By the mid-1980s, the federal budget deficit had displaced inflation as the biggest economic issue facing the nation. The United States government was more than $2 trillion in debt, and the Reagan administration was presiding over the largest yearly deficits in American history. Everybody agreed that this was bad. The President made speeches arguing for a constitutional amendment that would require that the budget be balanced, but he continued to draw up budgets with record deficits.

So the national debt continued to grow, alarming one and all. Congressmen and newspaper editorials cried out, "Just imagine what a pickle *you* would be in if, year after year, your household spent more than it took in. Would you not soon be on the road to ruin?" People listened to this and nodded their heads. They knew that they would indeed be sunk if they spent more than they earned, so they assumed that that was also the case for the government, which didn't even have the option of a garage sale to fall back on.

While the deficits are troubling, this analogy is false.

The government is not a household, and its finances should not be compared to yours or mine.

For one thing, it is perfectly appropriate for some current government liabilities to be passed on to future generations. The United States of America is a going concern. It will be around for a long time, and a significant part of federal spending reflects that. Much of the money the government pays out every year is not poured down a rathole but invested in the future. If the government borrows money to build a water-purification system, say, it may add $1 billion to the current-year deficit. But the government has created an asset that is worth $1 billion. The asset balances the liability. And when commentators profess pity for unborn generations of Americans who will come into the world owing a portion of a huge debt that they did not help incur, think twice before you cry for them. They're going to get to drink the water, aren't they? (Admittedly, it is harder to make this kind of argument on behalf of a toilet seat for which the Pentagon has spent $1,000.) Just imagine what benefits our grandchildren may reap from the money the government borrows today to finance the space program or medical research into cancer or heart disease.

Unlike other major nations, the United States does not designate part of its government spending as "investment," but it is. Long-term assets created by the government— roads, dams, airports, public transportation systems, information and communications networks, police stations, post offices, weather satellites, and more—contribute to the smooth and profitable functioning of the American economy and will do so for years to come.

Even expenditures on nondurable items may be thought of as investments. Money for education or health care for children, for example, is an investment in human capital. A child who grows up healthy and well educated is likely to make a future economic contribution to the nation.

And there is another, more immediate, benefit to government outlays. Think about what happens when Uncle Sam spends a dollar. The President has requested and Congress has appropriated funds for, say, White House office supplies. One dollar is allocated for a refill for the President's pen. Sure enough, the pen runs dry. The General Services Administration runs over to an office supply wholesaler and buys a refill for a dollar. The wholesaler is glad to have the dollar; it's part of a profitable government contract that has enabled his business to expand. He puts the dollar in his checking account and writes a paycheck to a new employee he's just hired. The employee is glad to have the dollar; she's been out of work for a while. She puts the dollar toward a new car she's been needing. Now a Ford dealer has the dollar. He's been having a good year and he decides to splurge. He takes the wife and kids to Disney World. Pretty soon Donald Duck (a young woman in a huge duck head) has the dollar. . . . You get the idea. Through this "multiplier effect," a single dollar goes a long way. It becomes, in effect, many dollars, subsidizing businesses, workers, factories, cartoon characters, etc. If that one dollar had never been spent, many Americans would be a dollar poorer. If the billions of dollars the government pumps into the economy were suddenly withdrawn, the economy would be knocked into a tailspin. A lot of people would have to go back to inspecting the sunshine and whittling sticks.

Of course, those dollars would go just as far if they originated with a private party; they don't have to come from the government. But sometimes private parties don't have many dollars. The economy is in recession. Times are hard. Nobody is going to Orlando. During such periods, governments routinely leap in and start to spend. Economic recovery requires it. Government spending also soars during wars, when concern about deficits takes a back seat not to economic recovery but to national survival.

One useful way to look at the national debt is to compare it to the Gross National Product (the total value of all goods and services produced by the economy in a given year). In 1945, at the end of World War II, the American national debt actually exceeded the Gross National Product. The ratio of debt to GNP has never been so high, before or since. In 1987, by contrast, the national debt was about 54 percent the size of the GNP.

So the size of the national debt today is not unprecedented. (In dollars, it is bigger than ever, but all dollar numbers have grown over the years because of inflation.) What is disturbing about the current debt is that it is growing at a time when we are in neither a war nor a recession. Historically, the deficit has shrunk during such periods. (One could argue, however, that Cold War military spending has put the American economy on a permanent war footing.)[1]

The greatest danger posed by an expanding deficit is that, to finance it, the government must compete in financial markets with businesses looking for loans. Competition for loans drives up interest rates and may make it difficult for businesses to finance expansion. Economic growth may be slowed.

The relationship between interest rates and prosperity was one element in the dramatic stock market collapse of October 1987. Historically, stock prices fall when interest

---

[1] One ought also to balance the federal government deficit against the substantial *surpluses* accumulated in recent years by state and local governments.

rates rise. That is because investors fear high interest rates may inhibit corporate growth and because investors can themselves profit from high interest rates by buying bonds instead of stocks. In the months preceding the October 1987 crash, interest rates had risen. In a departure from history, stock prices rose as well—until October. Following the crash, the Federal Reserve System immediately took moves designed to lower interest rates.

The government also reacted to the market collapse by allowing the dollar to fall against other currencies. A falling dollar makes foreign goods more expensive to American consumers (and American goods cheaper to foreign consumers). The move was designed to reduce the high United States trade deficit, which had been a matter of concern for some time. But the trade deficit was by no means an unmixed evil. It was true that foreign manufacturers were selling more goods in America than American manufacturers were selling abroad. It was also true that American workers in industries like clothing and cars were losing jobs because of the sales of foreign clothing and cars in this country. But foreign goods made cheap by a strong dollar helped keep inflation down. And most American customers enjoyed buying and using these low-cost imports.

THE UPWARD TREND

In the end, there is not much an individual can do about most of the cycles the economy goes through. You should always keep an eye on interest rates, of course, and consider moving some of your investment dollars from stocks to bonds when interest rates go up. You might also want to buy real property. at the start of an inflationary period. The tricky part there is figuring out exactly when an inflationary period is starting. If you make your move from cash to hard assets late—as many people invariably do—you may find that prices have already been jacked up to what will turn out to be their peaks, and you will be stuck with some extremely expensive rare stamps. (Since the odds are that you will *not* be able to predict the start of the next period of high inflation, it is a good idea to always keep some share of your net worth in the kind of assets that will rise with inflation. In investing, diversification is always a sound strategy.)

The most important thing to keep in mind is that, in the long run, all the cycles even out and the economy moves ahead. Wealth is still being created in this country, despite the cyclical ups and downs and all the momentary panics. In the short run, things may look shaky, but, in the long run, things tend to advance. And we all live our lives in the long run.

It therefore little profits most individuals to worry about this year's, or even this decade's, financial crisis. And it little profits a prudent investment strategy to be overly concerned with the short term either. You should invest as if the country will continue to prosper, as it has prospered, over the long run, for more than two hundred years. If *that* trend collapses, and the country enters a terminal Great Depression, you will lose everything. But you will have lost everything no matter what you did.

I refuse to believe that America is on its last legs. I know all about the short-term uncertainties and the gloomy pundits who see the specter of 1929 around every corner. I've seen them come and I've seen them go. But the fundamentals are strong. The spirit of enterprise constantly renews itself.

There is a happy symmetry between individual investments and national economic health. Through the act of investing, individuals link their fortunes to American industry and profit as it profits. Simultaneously, through the act of investing, individuals make it *possible* for American industry to grow. The American economy requires savings and investment to finance its development and expansion. Without the dollars individuals put into stocks and bonds and other securities, America would grind to a halt. Those investment dollars finance the American future. As that future comes to pass, it will amply repay those who have invested in it.

INDEX